STAIRLIFT TO HEAVEN 4

Still Hanging On

Terry Ravenscroft

A RAZZAMATAZZ PUBLICATION

For my children Gail, Carol-Ann and Dean.

ABOUT THE AUTHOR

The day after Terry Ravenscroft threw in his mundane factory job to become a television comedy scriptwriter he was involved in a car accident which left him unable to turn his head. Since then he has never looked back.

Before they took him away he wrote scripts for Les Dawson, The Two Ronnies, Morecambe and Wise, Alas Smith and Jones, Not the Nine O'Clock News, Ken Dodd, Roy Hudd, and several others. He also wrote the award-winning BBC radio series Star Terk Two.

Born in New Mills, Derbyshire, in 1938, he still lives there with his girlfriend, Divine Bottom (in his dreams).

ALSO BY TERRY RAVENSCROFT

PREFACE

Since I wrote Stairlift to Heaven 3 - Almost There, my wife Delma 'The Trouble' has died.

Delma had the nicest smile you ever saw and a disposition to match. I was twenty-one and she was nineteen when we met. I loved her from the moment I first saw her and will go on loving her until the day I die. Well intentioned friends, some of whom have suffered a similar loss, say that eventually I will get through the pain of her death and come out the other side. I won't, for me there is no other side; if there is indeed light at the end of tunnel it must be coming from a five watt bulb painted black. So I just to get on with the rest of my life as best I can.

I could always make Delma laugh. I think it's what she liked about me. I made her laugh the day before she died, with one of my silly jokes. I'm glad about that.

One day, soon after she left me, I found myself envying people who believed in God and the hereafter. But not for long; I soon recalled that people who believe in God and Heaven must by definition also believe in the Devil and Hell, and from what I've seen of some people who profess a belief in God they won't be ending up in a place redolent with the scent of May blossom and roses, rather the stench of fire and brimstone. Adolf Hitler believed in God. I don't think I need say any more. Right, that's the sad stuff off out of the way, so it's on with the show.

Although I will mourn The Trouble for evermore I wouldn't be completely honest if I didn't admit that I have benefited in many ways since she died. (I can't bring myself to say 'passed away', 'passed', or whatever other trite expressions people use to dress up the word 'died'. One man said to me *"I'm sorry to hear your wife has passed."* Perhaps unfairly I replied that she hadn't 'passed', she wasn't a footballer or a rugby player, she was a woman, the woman I loved.

Some of the benefits are:-

I no longer have to wait for her forever, as was always the case whenever we went out together. So no more standing by the front door tapping my foot impatiently while she changes her shoes for the fourth time, before finally changing them for the ones she put on in the first place.

I no longer have to listen to the sound of her spoon slowly scraping the complete circumference of her cereal bowl before each mouthful whilst taking about three days to eat a bowl of cornflakes.

I no longer have to listen to her simply repeat the last word she said - leaving me no wiser than when I asked - whenever I hadn't heard her properly and asked her to repeat what she said, as in - *The Trouble: "Do you want anything from the shops?" Me: "What?" The Trouble: "Shops."*

I no longer have to put up with her total inability to sort more than six of my socks into three matching pairs.

I no longer have to put up with her buying every household product that incorporates an aerosol spray. Out house was always full of them. If I'd put them all in the coffin with her when she was cremated the resulting explosion would have demolished the entire cemetery.

I no longer have to listen to her telling me to stop talking to the TV set and calling some 'celebrity' or other a self-regarding no talent twat, or whatever. (More of this later.)

I no longer have to listen to her moaning at me when I shout at the telly. (More of this too.)

I have benefited in many other ways following The Trouble's death, too many to mention. I would, however, willingly give up every one of them, and more besides, for a single minute more of her company.

My best friend Atkins's wife Meg also died, last June, the month after The Trouble, and from the same horrible disease, cancer. So Atkins and I are in the same boat, up shit creek, if not without a paddle then without much hope of ever navigating ourselves out of it. Consequentially we see even more of each other than we used to. This, a source of company apart, is not necessarily a good thing; a little of Atkins goes a long way. However, too much Atkins is far, far better than no Atkins at all. And on the occasions it isn't, well, it keeps me on my toes.

I am now at an age, as is Atkins, that whenever you are asked your birthday you don't give your age but hopefully, and perhaps tempting providence, state the age you will be on your next birthday. *"I'll be eighty next birthday."* It occurs to me that small children do the same: a two-year-old when asked his or her age will always say they're three next birthday. This nonsense stops at around the age of ten and kicks in again when you're in your late sixties. It is another example of going back to your childhood once you've grown old, along with coming into the world bald and toothless and departing it in the same state, having insufficient control of your bladder and bowels, talking gibberish and dribbling, and becoming dependent on some form of wheeled conveyance to get around. Fortunately I have managed up until now to resist telling people *"I'll be eighty next birthday"* and am still managing to get about without recourse to a wheelchair. (Although I would fail, at least to some extent, in the bald, toothless, talking gibberish and insufficient control of bladder and bowels departments.)

After The Trouble died I thought I would never write again. I didn't think I could, nor did I want to, I just didn't see the point. They say time is a great healer. Well if it is it's taking its time about it; since her death I have healed, at most, about one per cent. However the one per cent of me that has healed has enabled me to write this, my fourth Stairlift book.

Terry Ravenscroft. 29th September 2017.

April 2 2017. *HEART MONITOR.*

"I'd like to make an amendment to the form I filled in when you fitted me with a heart monitor," said Atkins to the nurse.

"I'm afraid that's too late," the nurse replied, all starched hat and efficiency. "It will be in Medical Records by now." She said this with a finality that spelled out in no uncertain terms that once something was in Medical Records only an all-out assault by the SAS assisted by a SWAT team would be capable of removing it.

Atkins scowled at her and looked to me for assistance. I shrugged in despair. Atkins sighed deeply, took a deep breath, steeled himself and muttered, "In that case I would like to apologise."

Months earlier, as the last step in a three-procedure check up on the condition of my heart, I had to wear a heart monitor. (The other procedures were an angiogram, which resulted in the good news that my coronary arteries are still in good nick following bypass surgery in 2014, and a scan of my repaired aorta, which had burst about eighteen months ago. Sometimes I feel like a walking miracle.) After a nurse had fitted me with the monitor and offered instructions on how to cope with the inconvenience of wearing it - on going to bed, when washing, showering, et cetera - she handed me a form. "Write down what you were doing during the twenty-four hours you're wearing it and how long you were doing it for."

"You mean like 'walking, two-o-clock to three-o-clock, watching the telly, three till four', that sort of thing?"

"Spot on."

I glanced at the form and after a moment said, "I bet you don't get too many people putting 'masturbating' down, do you?"

She blushed but couldn't hold back a laugh. "Cheeky," she said, wagging a finger at me. "Bring it back with the monitor, same time tomorrow."

The following day I handed in the form at the appointed hour.

The nurse ran her eyes down the list of the things I had been doing since I last saw her.

"I haven't put everything down," I said coyly.

She smiled. "Perhaps it's a good job."

A couple of days later I mentioned the incident to Atkins.

"Did you?" he said unbelievingly. Then, with envy, "I wish I'd said it, I'd have loved to have said that."

"So what's stopping you?"

"What?"

"Well you've got a heart condition, haven't you." Like me Atkins has undergone heart surgery. "Just tell your doctor you're worried, throw a few symptoms at him and say that just to be on the safe side you'd like that twenty-four hour monitor thing; he'll go along with it just to get rid of you if I know my doctors."

"You reckon?"

That was about two months ago. This morning he was round at my house red in the face and steaming. "They're only threatening to take me to court!"

"Who are?"

"The bloody hospital. They sent me this!" He read off the letter he had received. *"'Our staff has the right to go about their employment without being subjected to physical or verbal abuse. Therefore....'"* He broke off. "And more of the same sort of shite. Can you credit it?"

"What have you done to deserve that?"

"Nothing."

"You must have done something."

After a moment Atkins shrugged. "It must be to do with when I went to have the heart monitor fitted and said to the nurse 'I bet you don't get many people putting 'masturbating' down'"

This was news to me. "You never told me you'd been too?"

"I suppose I might have expected something like this from the way she looked at me when I said it," said Atkins, as much to himself as to me.

I commiserated with him. "You obviously didn't get the same nurse I did. What did she look like?"

"About fifty, fat, tits round her waist."

"You didn't then. Mine was about twenty-five, blonde, nice figure."

"She was on the other station. I avoided her on purpose; well, she'd already heard the masturbation joke hadn't she, I didn't want to risk her saying 'I've heard that one before'."

"You'd have been better off taking the risk by the sounds of it."

Atkins scowled. "Well I know that now, don't I."

I thought about it for a moment. "You see if you'd put 'Masturbating' on the form you'd probably have been all right."

"What?"

"Well in that case it couldn't have been construed as verbal abuse; I mean if you had *intended* to masturbate it could be argued that you were merely implying there was a likelihood of you putting it down on the form."

Atkins considered this. "Hmm....Yes, I see what you mean."

"Your best bet is to go back to the hospital, explain to them, and ask for the form back."

"What if they won't let me have it?"

"Then you'll just have to apologise. That might do the trick."

Atkins was not happy. "Apologise?"

"I don't see any alternative if you want to keep out of the courts."

Atkins dwelled on this for a moment then said, "No. No you're right."

"I'll come with you," I said. I wasn't going to miss it for anything.

Atkins suddenly realised something. "Bloody hell! Bloody hell, Razza. *I could have put it down at the time!*"

"What?"

"I really *did* masturbate. Christina Trevanion was on *Bargain Hunt*; she always gets me going."

"Oh cruel, cruel irony," I said, coming over all Shakespeare. I had a thought. "What did you put down on the form?"

"Jogging, one-o-clock till ten past'."

We don't yet know if Atkins's apology will get him off the hook. Time will tell.

****

April 7 2017. *THE PARK UNDER THE TOWN.*

New Mills, the small town in the Peak District of Derbyshire in which I have lived happily all my life without ever wishing to live anywhere else, is the proud possessor of an outstanding riverside park. Known as 'The Park under the Town', it really is 'under' the town, having been formed in the ice age when the ice melted and left in its wake, cleaved through the sandstone, a quite spectacular one hundred feet deep gorge. Within the gorge - also known as 'The Torrs'- are two rivers, a waterfall, a derelict but fully intact cotton mill built during the Industrial Revolution, the ruins of six more cotton mills of various sizes, a dozen road, rail and foot bridges, and the *Millenium Walkway*, a one hundred and sixty yards long bridge which, suspended forty feet above the river, clings precariously to the cliff face. In verdant areas amongst the scant remains of the cotton mills are bluebells and daffodils and buttercups and daisies, in season, along with discarded condoms, whatever the season, casually deposited there by nocturnal lovers. (One day I saw, draped on a toadstool, a condom in an attractive shade of pink, the business end of it shaped like a pig's head. It looked quite striking against the brown sandstone of the cliffs.)

The Park is well worth seeing, and is visited by lots of out-of-towners from the nearby cities of

Manchester and Sheffield and beyond. But not, it saddens me to say, by the vast majority of the townsfolk, most of whom would probably only venture into its depths in the company of others, and only then if the party were led by Bear Grylls wielding a machete. (If you were to blindfold the aforementioned nocturnal lovers, lead them into The Torrs and remove their blindfolds, most of them wouldn't have the slightest idea as to where they were.)

I often walk down there and today, when I reached the part where the River Goyt is joined by the River Sett before carrying on as the Goyt and eventually joining the River Mersey at Stockport, and thence to Liverpool and the sea, I came across a party of about forty or so schoolchildren, girls and boys, grouped around their teacher, listening to her as she regaled them with the history of the area. They were typical 2017 teenagers. Many of the boys had haircuts half one side of the head shaved close to the bone the other half hair left lank. When I was their age if my mother had told me I had to have my hair cut like that I'd have ran away from home. (In my class at school we had a boy whose father used to attend to his son's hairdressing needs by shaving his head all over apart from a fringe that started at the very front of his head and finished just above his eyes. We used to call him 'Piebald' (after piebald pony) and whenever his dad had newly cut his hair word quickly spread through the school, *"Piebald's had a haircut, Piebald's had a haircut!"* At playtime the entire school would converge on poor Piebald for a gawp at his dad's latest tonsorial masterpiece and to point at him and jeer, to his great discomfort. He spent more time bunking off than anyone else in the entire school. Sadly I can't say that anyone, me included, felt the slightest sympathy for him, but children then, as now, can be very cruel.)

Not to be outdone in the weird look stakes, all the girls sported eyebrows that looked for all the world as though someone had shaved off their eyebrows and ironed on two slugs in their place.

Two of the boys were holding hands. It didn't surprise me; if a lad had been wearing a dress it wouldn't have surprised me. Not in the enlightened, inclusive times we now live in. When I was a child you were either a boy or a girl, you didn't get to choose your own gender from about the age of two as you can nowadays.(I must confess that all this alternative gender business leaves me quite confused. When I first heard the term LGBT I thought it was a new type of gas, perhaps similar to LPG gas, and not the initial letters of Lesbian, Gay, Bi-sexual and Transgender - although, thinking about it, I suppose that some lesbians, gays, bi-sexuals, and transgenders might well feel that their lifestyle is a bit of a gas.)

Always eager to add to my knowledge I stopped to listen to the teacher's words. As I tuned in a thought occurred to me. I turned to the boy nearest me, a lad of about fourteen with a watch as big as an alarm clock strapped to his wrist. (Although I didn't hold this against him; at his age I was the proud owner of a Mickey Mouse watch, the 'must have' in watches at the time.) Giving him a friendly smile I said, "Would you like to impress your teacher, son?" He looked at me suspiciously, as children do nowadays on being spoken to by a complete stranger. Then, thankfully judging that my smile wasn't the opening gambit of a paedophile, he shrugged and said, "Might. What do I have to do?"

"Attract the attention of your teacher and say to her, 'Miss, where the two rivers meet, is that what is known as a confluence?'"

The boy nodded agreement, put his hand in the air and waved. "Miss. Miss."

"Yes, Brad, what is it?" the teacher replied, peering over her granny glasses.

"Where the two rivers meet, is that what's known as a confluence?"

The teacher's face was blanker than a whiteout in the Arctic. "Is it?"

I gave her the benefit of the doubt, English Language perhaps not being the strongest subject of a history teacher. Or perhaps she was their geography teacher? I asked the boy. "What subject does your teacher take you for?"

"Miss Kowalski? English."

"Miss Kowalski?"

"She's a Pole."

"Dancer," said the cheeky-faced boy standing next to him.

So we have a Polish woman, who doesn't know the definition of the word confluence, teaching English to our children. And we wonder why it is that they struggle to get a job when they eventually leave school. I shook my head sadly and continued my walk.

****

April 10 2017. *THE BOYS FROM THE BLACK STUFF.*

About thirty years ago there was an excellent series on television called *The Boys from the Blackstuff*, about a gang of men who laid tarmac for a living. I had a visit from such a gang yesterday. The tarmac-layers in the TV series were Liverpudlians, as tricky as a barrowload of monkeys, but then the profession of tarmac-laying seems to attract the dodgy no matter which part of Great Britain they hail from. These men were an Irish version of the breed.

The one who called at my door tipped his hat in deference and said, "Good morning to you, sir. I just happened to be passing and couldn't help noticing your drive could do with re-tarmacing. Now me and my two boys have just finished a job not a million miles from here, so we have, and fortunately for you we have enough tarmac left over to do you a fine job."

To be honest I had been aware for some time that the drive could do with re-tarmacing, but I'd never got round to organising it. By now, probably thirty years after it had been laid, it had a few undulations in it, no doubt due to a bit of subsidence over the years. Near the entrance a small puddle formed whenever it rained. One day the postman, having trod in it whilst not looking where he was going, said I ought to get it seen to, it was a hazard. I told him it wasn't as big a hazard as my forgetting about his tip when Christmas came round and he never mentioned it again.

"How much is it going to cost me?" I said to

the Irishman.

"I could do it for eight hundred pounds. That's with your old tarmac prepared so as the new will stick to it good and proper, a generous inch and a half of new tarmac laid on top and rolled as flat as Titless Mary. (I didn't ask who Titless Mary was, possibly a saint, the man being Irish.) It's only that cheap as it's left over from the job we've just finished - you can come and inspect the quality of the workmanship if it takes your fancy. If we don't lay the tarmac today it will be wasted, you understand."

Eight hundred pounds didn't seem a bad price; The Topleys up the road had their drive re-tarmaced last year, the same size drive as mine, and it had cost them thirteen hundred. However I am wise to the ways of tarmac-layers who turn up on people's doorsteps with a load of tarmac supposedly going begging; I had heard that often you don't get what you've paid for, and even if you do it could well be a shoddy job. Could I, then, trust them to do a decent job? Fortunately I could; when I had first learned of the shenanigans these people get up to I had wondered how I could guarantee a proper job at the agreed price if ever I was put in the same position and in the meantime had come up with a suitable tactic. Accordingly I said, "The job is yours."

The Irishman took my hand in his, gave it a firm shake and looked at me keenly. "It will have to be notes; I don't do cheques or credit cards."

I gave him a man-of-the-world look. "I wouldn't have expected anything else; the black economy and that?"

"What's that you say?"

"The black economy. Cash. No need to trouble the income tax and VAT people is there? Yes, notes will be fine. I'll go to a cash machine while you're on with the job. What do I call you by the way?"

"Paddy. Or Pat. I'm happy with either. And what do I call you?"

"Sir."

"I'll be back with my two boys and the blackstuff in a flash, sir."

I got back from the cash point to find a lorry with a load of tarmac parked outside and three men hard at work, Paddy and two younger likenesses of him. Paddy noticed me as I worked my way precariously up the lawn by the side of the drive on my way back indoors. He paused in his labours and came over. "Quality work, as you can see, sir, quality work." A sweep of his arm invited me to take in their workmanship.

I glanced at it. It looked to be well up to par. I congratulated Paddy. "Titless Mary must have been very flat indeed."

"I believe she was, sir, I believe she was."

I shook a cautionary finger. "Now I don't want you coming to me later and telling me it's turned out to be a bigger job than you expected and it will be another two hundred quid."

"I won't be doing that, sir. Not at all, sir, you can count on that."

"And I don't want you laying the tarmac any thinner than you said you would."

Paddy looked affronted. "You can see with

your own eyes how thick we're laying it, so you can."

"Yes but that's while I'm here, isn't it? But not to worry, I shall be popping out every few minutes to satisfy myself you're keeping to your word."

"Oh we'll be doing that, sir, to be sure we will."

I made to go but then, if as an afterthought, I said, "Laying tarmac must be a very interesting job?"

"Oh it is, sir, it is indeed."

I shrugged and looked very wan. "Much more interesting than my job."

He looked surprised. "You still turn a hand do you? I would have thought an old gentleman such as yourself would be retired by now."

"I'm a lot younger than I look. The pressures of my profession have aged me prematurely."

"So what do you do then?"

"I'm an income tax inspector."

Paddy didn't exactly go white but his ruddy complexion immediately paled several shades.

"And I know who you are, too," I said. "It's on your lorry. 'Pat Finucane & Sons' Along with your address. I have also noted the registration number of your lorry, should I need one of my colleagues or the DHSS or the DVLC to track you down. So I'll let you and your lads get on with it then." I threw him a smile and left them to it.

In fact I did pop out from time to time to check on their work and it was well up to scratch, but I really didn't think I had to.

My drive is looking excellent. I have every confidence it will stay that way.

****

April 20 2017. *A RACIAL SLUR.*

Searching for a little light relief to ease the livelong day Atkins and I went along to a police station this morning. However, as both of us have had a bit of trouble with the local constabulary in the past, we took my problem to a Stockport branch of the force, where we are, as yet, unknown.

"I've got a problem I'd like you to help me with if at all possible," I said to the constable at the desk.

"Yes?" he said, showing about as much interest as would a dead poodle in Stephen Hawking's *A Brief History of Time.*

"You see I'm a bit worried about calling my friend Mr Atkins a monkey." I indicated Atkins. "This is the gentleman in question."

The constable eyed me quizzically. "You're worried about calling him a monkey?"

"I sometimes do," I explained. "You know, as in 'You *cheeky* monkey, you'."

"I'm very often a bit cheeky," smiled Atkins. "It's my nature."

"It's never worried me in the past," I continued, "but now, in the light of all the recent hoo-ha with the footballer, it worries me greatly."

"What hoo-ha is that then?"

"Ross Barkley," said Atkins. "The Everton

midfielder."

"You are familiar with the case?" I said.

The constable shook his head. "I don't follow football. Into MMA myself."

"MMA?"

"Mixed Martial Arts. Cage fighting."

"A more appropriate pastime than football for a policeman, I would say; Karate, judo, taikwondo and such," said Atkins knowledgeably. "I mean I can't see you having much joy trying to football an armed robber into submission. All right, making full use of your soccer skills you would be able to kick him and head him but there are times when nothing but a deft karate chop to the kidneys will quieten an armed robber down a bit, in my experience."

The constable looked sharply at Atkins. "What?"

Atkins, as can easily happen, and happens more often than I would like, had got himself carried away by the drama of the situation and departed from our prepared script. I swiftly got the conversation back on course. "Allow me to enlighten you as to the salient facts in the case, Constable. The main one being that Kelvin MacKenzie, one of the Sun newspaper's columnists - in fact at one time that publication's editor if my memory serves me correctly - compared Mr Barkley to a gorilla."

"And?"

"Well it's as good as calling him a nigger, isn't it," said Atkins.

"And you can't go around calling people niggers," I added. "What? You'd get locked up.

You people would see to that I'm sure."

"Right."

"Unless you happen to be black," said Atkins. "Then it's all right to call someone a nigger. You hear it all the time, *'You're my nigger, bro, you're my nigger'* It's a sort of form of affection I think, a sort of brotherly love."

I took over. "However, white people can't say *'You're my nigger'*. It is the sole reserve of black people." I paused for a moment and looked thoughtful. "It's always seemed unfair to me. I mean white people don't go around saying *'You're my Caucasian, bro, you're my Caucasian'*, do they? And I personally would be the last person to raise objections if a black man said to me, *'You're my Caucasian'*. Yet the shit would hit the fan if I said *'You're my nigger'* to him."

The constable, showing the first signs of interest, said, "So this Ross Barkley bloke, he's black then?"

"Well not that you'd notice. In fact he looks as white as I am. He looks whiter than Mr Atkins, but then Mr Atkins has just spent a couple of weeks in the Canary Islands. But apparently Ross Barkley's grandfather is Nigerian."

"Making what Kelvin MacKenzie said a racial slur," said Atkins. "Which, subsequently, led to the Sun being forced into making a grovelling apology."

"And rightly so," I added.

The constable thought about this for a moment before saying, "Well this is all very interesting I'm sure, but what has it got to do with you being worried about calling Mr Atkins a monkey?"

"Well it's the same as calling him a nigger, isn't it; applying the Ross Barkley principle."

"Why is it?"

"Well my great, great grandfather was Fijian," said Atkins. "A Fijian chief in fact."

"Clearly making him part black," I added. "Just as Ross Barkley's Nigerian grandfather makes Barkley part black. And thus...." I spread my arms in a 'so there you have it' gesture.

The constable looked more closely at Atkins and said to me, "You'd never know his grandfather was a Fijian, would you."

"You'd never know Ross Barkley's grandfather was a Nigerian," I replied. "But that didn't stop Kelvin MacKenzie and the Sun getting into a shitload of trouble."

The constable nodded. "Right."

"It's not of course that I *mind* being called a monkey," said Atkins.

"No?"

"Not at all."

The constable mulled this over for a moment or two, then said, puzzled. "So why are you here then?"

"For some advice. You see it could conceivably happen that when I call Mr Atkins a monkey a black man might overhear me. And, if he knew that Mr Atkins was one sixteenth Fijian - and Mr Atkins doesn't make any secret of his being part Fijian, in fact he's quite proud that his great, great grandfather was Chief Umumma of Fiji - the black man might feel that *he himself* has been racially abused."

Atkins nodded agreement. "Even though the fifteen sixteenths non-Fijian white part of me hasn't."

"So, bearing all this in mind, I want some advice as to what to do in future reference to calling Mr Atkins a monkey."

The constable struggled with this. Then, after possibly having an epiphany judging by the sudden expression of delight on his face, he said, with Solomon-like wisdom, "*Never* call him a monkey. Then there won't be a problem."

"Never call him a monkey?" I said, a bit annoyed. "Never call him a monkey? Is that the best you can do?"

"I told you we should have gone to Relate," said Atkins, and we left smartly before we got ourselves into trouble.

****

May 8 2017. *A CANVASSER CALLS.*

A General Election was announced the other week, bringing in its wake the constraint that until Election Day and beyond I will not be able to watch the first ninety-five per cent of the TV news or read the first five or six pages of my newspaper. I have also had to dispense with my radio channel of preference, Radio Five, and have tuned in my set to TalkSport for the duration.

The political parties represented in my constituency are the Monster Raving Loony Party, the Conservative Monster Raving Loony Party, the Labour Monster Raving Loony Party, the Liberal Democrat Monster Raving Loony

Party, the Green Monster Raving Loony Party, and the UKIP Monster Raving Especially Loony Party. I will of course not be voting - I can't recall precisely when I last voted but I think Pitt the Younger was Prime Minister - but that, of course, will not stop election canvassers arriving unannounced and unwanted on my doorstep. (I was going to vote in the Europe Referendum but as you couldn't cast your vote for 'Remain in Europe but only provided the French adopt all the new laws introduced instead of just the ones that suit them and Greece and Spain get their acts together' I didn't bother.)

Having slipped the custody of his carer the first of the canvassers fetched up this morning. I was ready for him. I don't know which candidate he was canvassing for, possibly a junior minister of the Department of Lying through our Teeth. He was wearing a royal blue rosette, which, not knowing the colours of the political parties, meant to me that he was either Conservative, Labour, Lib-Dem, UKIP, or an Everton supporter. If it turned out he was an Everton supporter he had no chance; being a lifelong supporter of Manchester United I hate Everton almost as much as I hate Liverpool.

My visitor put on an oily smile. "Good morning, sir. Can I count on your vote in the forthcoming election?"

"Only if you are quite mad."

Unabashed, he cocked an enquiring eyebrow in my direction. "Could I perhaps tempt you into changing your mind?"

"You could try, but it would be a hard and rocky road." I shrugged and spread my hands.

"But if it's a road you wish to set out on....?"

He added confidence to the oil in his smile. "I believe I can persuade you."

"Then you have my ear."

"Excellent." He took a deep breath. "Well then, clearly it is our intention...."

I broke in before he could start telling me that the old age pension would be going up to a thousand pounds a week, tax free, and that all male pensioners, if they preferred, would be free to sell their homes to the Government for ten million pounds and thereafter live rent free in a complimentary luxurious mansion complete with hot and cold running women. "How does your party stand on the Africa Position?" I said.

This stopped him dead in his tracks. His flummoxed expression made it plain that he knew not a thing about the Africa Position. But to be fair, neither did I, or even if there was an Africa Position. "Er.... well....I....I'll come to that later. But first, our policy on immigration, clearly, is...." he said, desperately throwing out a lifeline.

I threw it back. "I couldn't give a tinker's cuss about your policy on immigration. Besides, if you go back far enough in history we are all immigrants, unless you happen to be a descendant of the Picts. Which puts you out of the running as you are fair and balding, suggesting that your ancestors came from either one of the Scandinavian countries or Baldland. So as far as I am concerned we should let all people come and go as they wish. It is your stand on the Africa Position I am interested in, in particular the Lumshasa Position. How do you stand on it?"

His expression informed me that he knew even less about the Lumshasa Position than he did about the Africa Position. However he pulled himself together, looked to the heavens for inspiration, posed in thought and said slowly to himself, "Now let me see.... the Lumshasa Position....?"

Breaking into whatever lying thoughts he might have been having before he had the chance to form them into words I said, "It has to do with our missionaries out there. What do you think about the Missionary Position?" He looked at me open-mouthed, offering only a stupid grin in reply. I got tetchy with him. "Come come, man, when I asked the Labour candidate what he thought about the Missionary Position his reply was both illuminating and immediate."

"What did he say?"

"He said, *Is that the one lying down, man on top?*" Which, to be quite honest, wasn't the answer I was expecting; but at least he had an answer, which is more than can be said for you. However, forget that, how do you stand on the Amputee Position? Don't tell me - on one leg, somewhat precariously."

I let him go a couple of minutes later with the promise that I'd think about it.

Who would I vote for if ever I did vote? Certainly, I would be far more likely to vote for the parties led by Theresa May and Jeremy Corbyn than I would for the Lib Dems, a party headed by Tim Farron, an individual who, when it comes to the subject of homosexuality, firmly believed in the teachings of the bible until he realised it would cost him a few votes, at which point he promptly did an about face. And I would be more likely to vote for Jeremy Corbyn than I would for Theresa May; Corbyn generally talks shite but at least it's honest shite. I can't think I could ever vote for Theresa May, despite her laudable stance against Merkel and Juncker and the rest of the eurotwats who would do us down on the Brexit business; she looks too much like Margaret Thatcher for my liking.

In fact, given an ideal world, I would vote Labour, or Socialist or whatever the party is calling itself nowadays; for at heart I am a true Socialist. (As opposed to the Champagne Socialists initiated by Tony Blair and his dreadful cohorts, and continued by the one of the Miliband brothers who's a dead ringer for Wallace's dog Gromit. In my early twenties I read Robert Tressell's *The Ragged Trousered Philanthropists*. I was sold immediately. I have read it several times since; one of the times was when for some strange reason I had started to develop Conservative leanings. It cured me in five minutes. It is a book which spells out exactly what proper Socialism is. Set in the years around 1900, taking or leaving its politics it is a quite wonderful book, a harrowing but often hilarious story of working class life at that time as experienced by the writer himself. Everyone should read it at least once.

The only problem with it, and it is an insurmountable problem, is that the brand of Socialism preached by Robert Tressell just wouldn't work. In Tressell's Utopia no one is better, no one is more valuable, than anyone else. Everyone is equal. An ideal state of mind in an ideal state. And that is its undoing. Because all it takes is for one person to want more than someone else - and the world is full of these people - for the whole system to collapse. Shame; I wouldn't mind living in Utopia.

****

May 10 2017. *DAVID BECKHAM'S UNDERPANTS*

In conversation, what is the point of the word 'obviously'? If something is obvious there's no need to say it is obvious, so why bother? Yet people do, and all the time. (Indeed you would have about as much chance of hearing a footballer being interviewed without his saying 'obviously' at least once a sentence as you would of hearing him say 'Your throw' when the ball goes out of play.)

This being the case, some people might say, and I would be one of them, that it is perhaps no bad thing we have the word 'obviously', if only because footballers and most other people who make a living from football would be hard-pressed to put a sentence together without using it, along with its bedfellows 'you know', and 'at the end of the day'. *"How do you think you'll fare against Chelsea away, Jason?" "Well Chelsea are top of the Premier League, and we're, you know, second bottom of League Two, so obviously it's going to be, like, a difficult one for us at the end of the day."* The beautiful game it may be but it certainly doesn't trouble itself to use beautiful language.

Another word, even more beloved of football people, is 'massive'. To everyone involved in the game, players, managers, coaches, referees, programme presenters, fans, everything is 'massive'. There are no such words as huge, giant, colossal, enormous, immense, gigantic, gargantuan, monumental or titanic in a football person's vocabulary; everything, but everything, is 'massive'. It is a simple matter to prove this. Tune in to any football programme, especially radio talk-in shows, and I can guarantee that within a minute someone will have said 'massive'. I once counted seventeen massives in five minutes on BBC 1's *Football Focus*. Hang your heads in shame Mark Lawrenson and Alan Shearer. (When I first cottoned on to it, whenever I heard someone say 'massive' on the TV or radio I used to echo it with an impressive *"Massive!"* of my own. However I soon had to stop doing it as it was driving The Trouble up the wall.)

Perhaps I shouldn't complain too much though, especially as I recently had cause to be grateful for the football community's eccentric way of speaking.

Atkins had read somewhere that David Beckham only ever wears a pair of underpants once and then discards them. (I suppose they'll be the Calvin Klein type worn by the God David when he prostitutes himself in the pages of glossy magazines - the underpants that make it look as though along with his meat and two veg he has a couple of rolled-up pairs of hiking socks secreted in his crotch.) Seizing on this hardly surprising snippet of information as an opportunity to make some money - Atkins is always on the lookout for opportunities to make money, the more dubious the better - he wrote to Beckham asking him if, rather than throw the underpants away, he could pass them on to Atkins instead. My friend would then sell them on, passing on half the profits to a charity of Beckham's choice.

A couple of weeks later Atkins arrived on my front doorstep carrying a familiar-looking foolscap-size envelope. "Guess what?" he said, in a state of great excitement. "Beckham replied to my letter!"

I didn't need to 'guess what', I knew what. On the assumption that if the letter ever found its way to Beckham he would immediately bin it I wrote a reply to it myself, which I reproduce below. (Note: The spelling mistakes in the letter were for my own amusement, in the knowledge that they would go right over Atkins's head as, although he can be quite eloquent at times, he can't spell for toffee.) Atkins handed me the letter and I read it open-mouthed, as if for the first time.

Dear Richard

Massive thanks for your leter and saying that it's a bloody liberty I haven't been given a, like, nighthood yet. Obviously a nighthood means a lot to me. I mean, like I say, it would be massive to be, you know, addressed as Sir. Well obviously. Anyway I have arsked my good mate Prints Wiliam to put in a good word for me so no dowt I will be getin my nighthood in the next onners list which, will be unbeleevabel! But about you arsking me for my underpants. I mean I concidered it, obviously, but at the end of the day

I had to say no, as you will not be, like, surprised to lern that, what with me being, like, famous, it isn't the first time I've been arsked for my thrown away underpants. Obviously. I mean I have had to turn down a massive quantitty of, like, people, really massive. So I am afraid I must say no, wevver I, like, like it or not, as it wouldn't, you know, be fair to the massive quantitty of people all around the worlde who, you know, I have already had to, like, deckline at the end of the day. Well obviously. However, as you sound like a nice guy I enclose as a towken of my apreciation for your leter a pair of Victoria's knickers, which I nicked from her knicker draw.

Yours massively

I signed the letter 'David Beckham' after getting a copy of Beckham's autograph off the internet and practising it for a bit, and put it in the envelope along with a thong I bought from Marks, a red satin job with black lace trim (£12.99), then posted it to Atkins.

"So how about that then!" said Atkins, as happy as a sandboy let loose in the Sahara Desert with a bucket and spade. "And *you* said he'd never answer it."

"Well I didn't think he would. As David explained in his letter he must get lots of people asking him. Probably he looked fondly on you because you sympathised with him about his still not having a knighthood."

"But the *knickers*," said Atkins, unable to

contain himself. *"A pair of Victoria Beckham's knickers!"*

I looked inside the envelope. It was empty. "Where are they?"

"On ebay."

"What?"

"Soon, no doubt, to be with the lucky buyer." He rubbed his hands together. "Leaving me two hundred quid to the good."

"Two hundred quid?"

"I thought two fifty at first but I didn't want to push it."

"You must be joking," I scoffed. "Who in their right mind is going to give you two hundred quid for them? People weren't born yesterday, they could be anybody's knickers; how are you going to prove they're Victoria Beckham's?"

He grinned hugely, plucked the letter from my hand and caressed it close to his chest as lovingly as Fagin ever caressed his 'pretty things'. "Because I have providence, haven't I. I have authentication. I have proof they're the real thing, the genuine article. Not only that, in addition to the knickers, there is the bonus of David Beckham's autograph to take into consideration; I realise of course it isn't as valuable as a Beatles or Stones autograph but it must be worth a bob or two."

Atkins had himself a money spinner, of course. Selling the knickers on had never entered my head. And there was little doubt he would sell them; as he gleefully pointed out, he had providence, and to collectors providence is all.

In fact Atkins sold them later today to a man from Tunbridge Wells, probably an estate agent if I'm any judge of the sort of person in the market for a pair of Victoria Beckham's knickers.

****

May 13 2017. *INVICTUS.*

This week's *Sunday Times* reports that some of England's leading state schools are creating lists of up to a hundred classic poems and books which all pupils must study. Being armed with a wider knowledge than heretofore will help them enormously when they eventually go out into the big wide world to earn a living, it is claimed, plus a much wider vocabulary with which to put this knowledge to good effect. Amongst the poems they will be required to study are Alfred Lord Tennyson's *The Charge of the Light Brigade* (presumably to learn how to avoid doing bloody stupid things), John Donne's *No Man is an Island*, and William Ernest Henley's *Invictus*. Maybe to inspire us all to greatness the article reprinted *Invictus*, thus: -

Out of the night that covers me,
Black as the pit from Pole to Pole
I thank whatever gods may be
For my unconquerable soul

In the fell clutch of circumstance
I have not winced nor cried aloud
Under the bludgeoning of chance
My head is bloody, but unbowed

Beyond this place of wrath and tears
Looms but the Horror of the shade
And yet the menace of the years
Finds and shall find me unafraid

It matters not how strait the gate
How charged with punishments the scroll
I am the master of my fate
I am the captain of my soul.

A lot of words to say 'When things get a bit sticky it's up to you yourself to keep your pecker up and deal with it', in my humble opinion, but then who am I to argue with great poetry? In truth though, I can't see phrases such as *'Out of the night that covers me, Black as the pit from Pole to Pole'* being of much use to someone applying for a job as an accountant or a chartered surveyor, although I will concede that if the applicant were forced by the paucity of job opportunities today to seek employment at McDonalds or Burger King, as many university graduates are, *'Beyond this place of wrath and tears, Looms but the Horror of the shade'* might come in handy.

No, what today's school and university leavers need is poetry tailored to life beyond school as it is nowadays, a modern day *Invictus*, thus:-

From under the duvet that covers me I rise
Breakfast is cornflakes and a bacon roll
Two coffees, and thus fortified
I venture out to collect my dole

Ten years or more I filled my boots
With great poetry and great prose
But to what end? I have no job
And ever will I get one? Fuck knows

Should I have learned a trade, mayhap?
I must say yes, on balance
Than have sated myself on the classics and
Ended up on Job Seekers Allowance

I face the clerk across the counter
Will he sign me off, leave me in a hole?
He is the master of my fate
He is the captain of my dole

More apposite, methinks.

Of course there are lots of jobs available to school and university leavers. The problem is that most of the them are 'service' jobs such as cleaner or shelf-stacker, and therefore unworthy of consideration by a mollycoddled generation of young men and women brought up with a misguided sense of entitlement, and therefore unwilling to roll up their sleeves and accept such menial jobs whilst seeking the job they really want.

****

May 16 2017. *A CHEQUE FROM AMERICA.*

About twenty years ago your typical High Street bank was customer friendly. Nowadays banks are about as customer friendly as a prostitute with crabs. I was reminded of this on a recent visit to one. A bank, that is, not a prostitute. (Although the result would have been the same; they both fuck you.) The bank in question was our local Lloyds TSB, although I am sure what happened would have been the same at a branch of Barclays or NatWest; they all feed at the same trough.

A cheque from America had arrived, made out to my son Dean. Dean lives more or less permanently in various countries in the Far East, but has no permanent address there, so uses my address for any letters, catching up with them when he visits home from time to time. He had asked me to keep a look out for the cheque and when it arrived to pay it into his bank account, Dr D Ravenscroft. I tried to do this, two weeks ago. However the cheque was in US dollars, thus had to be 'negotiated' - a bank's expression for screwing you out of about five per cent of its value with little more effort on their part than the click of a computer mouse - into pounds sterling. What a performance! It went like this.

"I'd like to pay this cheque into my son's account." I handed the teller a note containing Dean's bank details along with the cheque.

The teller looked at the back of the cheque. "It isn't signed. He has to sign it."

"Oh, I see. Well I'm afraid that isn't possible, he's living in Vietnam."

"It still needs his signature."

"In that case I'll sign it for him."

"It has to *his* signature."

"I'll sign *his* signature then."

The teller gasped. "You can't do that! That's forgery! You can't go around forging signatures on cheques!"

"I'm not 'going around forging cheques', I'm forging, as you put it, one cheque, my son's."

The teller was not impressed. "It's still forgery.

I appealed to him. "Look, I'm paying money in, not trying to draw it out, I'm not trying to twist you, there's no danger of you losing out on this."

A waste of breath. "The cheque still needs to have Dean Ravenscroft's signature on it. His *proper* signature."

I glared at him. "And it will have." I held out my hand for the cheque.

"It has to be *his* signature."

"It will be."

"Which must match the copy of his signature we have on file."

"Shit," I said, but just enough under my breath for the teller not to hear me properly.

"And he'll need to fill in a form too."

When I got home I emailed Dean, told him what had happened and asked him to send me a copy of his signature. When it arrived, and using the forging skills I had honed when practising

David Beckham's autograph - there could be a new career for me here - I signed the cheque, filled in the form the teller had given me and signed that too. Then, instead of going back to the local Lloyds TSB, who already had me down as a wrong 'un, I took the cheque and form to another branch.

"I'd like to pay this cheque into my son's account."

The teller took the cheque and form, looked at the back of the cheque and scanned the form briefly. "You are the account holder?"

"Yes," I lied. I can lie with Nixon-like proficiency when the occasion demands.

"You are Doctor Dean Ravenscroft?"

"I am," I said, standing firm and trying to look doctorly.

"And this is your signature?"

"It is."

She turned to her computer, tapped away at the keyboard, looked at what she'd brought up on the screen, probably Dean's signature. She tapped another few keys then, puzzled, peered closely at me and said, "You look a bit old for forty-five?"

"I've had a hard life," I said, which I didn't think was a bad attempt at a reply on the spur of the moment.

"What?"

Then I cracked up.

She looked me up and down, as suspicious as a late night doner kebab. "You're *not* Dr Dean Ravenscroft are you?"

"Oh give me the bloody cheque back."

In the end, after waiting a couple of weeks to give the cheque time to supposedly get to Vietnam and back, my daughter Carol-Ann went back to our local Lloyds TSB to pay it in, under orders, if they wanted to know why I wasn't paying it in, to tell them I was in hospital due to stress brought on by banks treating their customers like shit. In the event this wasn't necessary as the teller accepted the cheque without demur. But what a pantomime.

****

May 23 2017. *A SAD DAY.*

It is twelve months to the day since Delma died. There is no grave to visit; like me she didn't fancy the idea of lying in a hole and letting the worms do their worst, so she was cremated. So there is no gravestone with her name on it. But there are flowers to be laid. Now, I set out with them - Delma loved flowers, our house was never without them.

Not far from where we lived, where I still live, is a place called Mousely Bottom. It is in a valley, the River Goyt meanders through it. There is a bench in Mousely Bottom, beside a large pond. There are numerous rhododendron bushes in the shadow of tall trees on three side of the pond, water lilies decorate it, small fish swim in it, it is the home of four terrapins, several mallards, sometimes a kingfisher or heron, in summer dragon flies flit about above the water. It is a quite beautiful spot, a microcosm of the English countryside. Some of Delma's and my grandson Daniel's ashes were scattered there. Mine will be joining them one day. The bench, a stout affair, was provided by Daniel's mates in his memory, and is in that spot in particular as it's where he often walked, sometimes with his mum. I have walked there with him. I thought the world of Daniel. I introduced him to good food, good wine, and good literature. He introduced me to Daniel. Centrally positioned on the back of the bench is a plaque with details of Daniel's date of birth and death along with etchings of a snake and a gecko, exotic reptiles being his great love. To its right is another plaque, added when Delma died. It says, simply, *'In memory of Delma Ravenscroft, Daniel's Nana, died May 23 2016'*. When I die there will be another plaque, to the left, for me, Daniel's grandad. I suggested to my daughter, Daniel's mum Carol-Ann, that perhaps we could put my plaque there now with the inscription *'Watch this space'* but she just laughed and told me not to be daft. But then I am a bit daft.

I go to the bench, lay flowers, sit on the bench awhile and think of the good times I shared with Delma.

I wrote the following poem in memory of her not long after she died.

Delma, my lovely wife has died
It will never seem quite right
That she is gone while I'm still here
I kiss her pillow each night

What will I do without her smile?
Will I ever feel all right?
I live in hope that the pain will go
I kiss her pillow each night

She gave me love since first we met
Not as a duty, but as a right
For that I'll be ever grateful
And kiss her pillow each night.

I say the poem silently to myself then dry my eyes and make my way home. There I have a pork pie (normally on my forbidden list) and a glass of good wine, to cheer me up a bit. The pie will later give me indigestion, but fuck it.

****

May 24 2017. *A PERFECT DAY.*

On my perfect day I awake around eight having spent an uninterrupted night's sleep for the first time in donkey's years. I will breakfast on two bacon barm cakes, one with brown HP sauce, the other not. Both will have been soaked in dip (the frying juices from the fat of the bacon, for those uninitiated in this culinary treat). Then two coffees, proper coffee not that instant muck.

I will then find myself in the Lake District, on the summit of Latrigg, a hill not a mountain. Behind me is the mass of Skiddaw, one of Lakelands highest peaks. In front of me I can see part of the outskirts of the small town of Keswick, nestling at the northernmost edge of Derwentwater. Beyond and surrounding the lake, like a tapestry, are the rest of the Lake District's highest peaks, Hellvellyn, Great Gable, Scaefell, Scaefell Pike. It is the best view I have ever seen in my life, or hope to see, a view I have seen several times, a view I will never tire of looking at. A friend of mine calls it 'God's Back Garden', but I don't believe in God so I call it my back garden.

Down from Latrigg I will go to a pub and lunch on moules marinières. It will be made with small French mussels, what the late and wonderful Keith Floyd called 'little black pearls', and with good reason. I like all seafood, lobster, crab, langoustines, but for me the humble mussel is the king of the sea and for my perfect day nothing else will do. I enjoy the moules marinières, mopping up the juices with chunks of crusty bread, and wash the lot down with a pint of the Lake District's own brew, Jennings Bitter. Magic.

I will then have an excellent seat at Old Trafford to watch Manchester United play Liverpool. I never usually watch my team play the scousers in case they lose. I can just about stand them losing to Liverpool but I don't want to see it. I don't much like watching United losing to any team. (I didn't see them win the European Cup against Bayern Munich as, like the great George Best, three minutes before the end, accepting that they would lose, we stopped watching it, George by leaving the stadium, me by switching off the telly). But United won't lose today, because today is my perfect day, today they will play Liverpool off the park and win 10-0.

All the Liverpool players will be wearing black curly-perm wigs and moan in unison *"You can't do that, that's just not on, la!"* every time United score. Several of the United goals will be own goals, for my extra enjoyment. Prawn sandwiches at half-time in honour of Roy Keane.

Following the game, as happy as Larry, only pausing for a while to jeer at the departing heartbroken Liverpool fans, I will make my way to a good Manchester restaurant for my evening meal. The restaurant has a Michelin star but tonight it won't need it to meet my requirements. I have experienced fine dining on a number of occasions - I once had the tasting menu at Michel Roux Junior's Le Gavroche, which cost over £200, (although I wasn't paying for it, I hasten to add - if I were ever to fork out £200 for food it would have to be for a week). However, for my perfect day I don't require the best that fine dining can offer, I don't want Stone Bass and Pastilla, Scented with Arabian Spices Fennel, Red Rice and Meat Jus or a Tarte Tatin de Légumes, Arc en Ciel de Purée, all I require from the chef is steak and chips - a juicy medium rare inch-thick ten ounce Aberdeen Angus sirloin steak and properly cooked chips, big, thick, fluffy on the inside, crisp and golden on the outside. Proper food. With it I will have just one large glass of a good red wine; there will be more, better wine, later at home.

My belly full I will make my way to the Manchester Arena where my evening's entertainment awaits. Just two acts. First up will be my favourite stand-up comedian Micky Flanagan. Micky is without doubt the funniest comedian I have ever seen, and I have seen many (and written for not a few). He doesn't tell jokes. It's all observation. But what observation. He is Peter Kay with bigger balls. Much of his talk is about himself, his wife, his friends, the interaction between men and women in general, the way men are, the way women are, the way kids are. No aspect of life is spared. He tells everything as it is. Nothing is off limits. As Micky says to the audience at one point in his *Out Out Tour* video, *"I bet you thought you were in for an easy ride, didn't you?"* If you have never seen him, make amends just as soon as you can.

Micky will do a couple of hours and then it will be music time. I have been a fan of rock music ever since it exploded onto the scene in the 1950's when I was about fourteen. I am a great fan of Pink Floyd, the Rolling Stones, the Kinks, the Eagles, REM, Blondie, more recently Pulp, Oasis, the Killers, Arcade Fire. But if I could only ever see one band again it would have to be the band that will complete the entertainment on my perfect day, Manchester's own, James. Fronted by Tim Booth, possessor of the most perfect voice in rock, the band's mastery of their guitars, drums, keyboards, strings and brass instruments produces the most together sound you have ever heard. I will be treated to intelligent lyrics that say something: *'After thirty years I've become my fears, I've become the kind of man I've always hated.' 'Those who find themselves ridiculous, Sit down next to me.'* You won't hear lyrics like that in a One Direction song. The back catalogue of James consists of well over a hundred songs and there's not a duff one amongst them. I can never listen to them, either live or on my car audio, without joining in. I will join in with all their songs tonight, from the anthemic 'Sit Down' through the brilliant 'Tomorrow' to the awesome 'Walk With You', as no doubt the rest of the audience will.

Finally home, having had my fill of the very best in beautiful scenery, great food, scintillating football and wonderful comedy and music, I will enjoy a bottle of fine burgundy before going to bed and having a wank. (No I won't, but that's what Micky Flanagan would say how he would end his perfect evening - I'll just have the burgundy and leave it at that.

****

May 25 2017. *A DAY IN MY LIFE.*

The time I awake to greet the new day depends on what time I go to bed the previous night, so it can be anything between one minute past midnight and 1.30 a.m. It is rarely later, and by no more than a half hour if it is. Why am I such an early riser? Because, like many men of advanced years, I suffer from nature's welcome to old age, a prostate gland problem, with the consequential trips to the lavatory for a pee that this terrible curse brings with it. Therefore I don't, like the majority of people, awake to greet the new day once, I awake to greet it half-a dozen times on average, at approximately one and a half hour intervals. After, say, the sixth greeting, around 8 a.m. I get up. I shower, I shave, sometimes I shampoo. I make my breakfast, always a grated apple, two chopped-up tinned pineapple rings, a dozen or so grapes, a generous dollop of yogurt, a few nuts, a squeeze of honey on top. I've been having the self-same breakfast every day for the last twenty years. It is quick to prepare, it's healthy, it's three of my 5-a-day, and once your bowels have become accustomed to it it doesn't add to global warming via gas emissions. Whilst enjoying my breakfast I listen to the radio. Although, as I mentioned about a month ago, it is at the moment permanently tuned in to the TalkSport channel until after the General Election, the news is not of football or cricket but of a bomb attack on the Manchester Arena during a pop concert. A heartbreaking start to the day. A real bummer.

Having breakfasted I take my seven heart attack prevention pills. I call them my Bee Gee pills. Staying Alive. Pilled up, I go to my computer about 9 a.m. I am sort of semi-retired these days but last night I decided that today would be a writing day and I always keep my word when it comes to writing; if I just waited until I was in the mood for it I would never write anything, since I am never in the mood for it. At the moment I'm writing either the book you are reading now, or *Cereal Killer*, a new novel in its early stages. I have often been asked if I enjoy writing. I don't. I hate it. For me, writing has always been difficult, by far the most difficult work I have ever done. I have dug ditches for a living, I have mixed plaster for a fast plasterer; neither were half as taxing, as tiring, as energy-sapping, as is writing. For me it can be likened to something akin to being a coal miner labouring at the coalface of a mine reluctant to give up its coal: a thesaurus is my mine, the words I extract from it the coal. I am having a hard day at the coalface at this very moment. What I *do* enjoy about writing, is having done it, having written something, having got it to the stage where I can't do anything further to make it any better, when it is finished. And I enjoy that more than anything else in the world. Except for sex of course.

After maybe a couple of hours at the coalface I set out for a walk along the Sett Valley Trail, a linear walk virtually on my doorstep. On the way I pick up my newspaper, the *Daily Telegraph*. On the Trail, I take in, once again, the lovely Derbyshire countryside. A jogger wearing earphones, drum-heavy music leaking ignorantly from them, eyes fixed straight ahead, passes by. Apart from getting some fresh air, why does he bother? If it's fresh air he wants he might just as well stay at home, open the window and jog on the spot.

As I'm walking along I let my mind wander. Soon it wanders to what I am currently writing. Another thing about writing: most people think it is done exclusively sat at a typewriter or computer keyboard. It isn't. At least mine isn't. Much of it is written whilst I'm doing other things; walking, eating, watching the telly, listening to the radio, soaking in the bath. Sooner or later something I see or hear sparks off an idea and I'm off 'writing' in my head again. I'm sure this is true of other writers.

Today, whilst my mind is wandering, it stops wandering and starts wondering when I see through the trees bordering the path a man having a dump. Has he been taken short? Is he homeless and has to take a shit wherever he can? Is it simply that he enjoys doing it *al fresco*? It takes all sorts, after all. *"Just off out for a dump,*

Love, won't be long, boil me an egg, a few soldiers would be nice." Initially I think he's just squatting there, hidden from view, trying to get a closer look at a woodpecker or a nuthatch, an unusual mushroom, a couple having it away. But soon he stands up, wipes his bum on a dock leaf, and pulls up his trousers, so he's been having a dump, no mistake. I note that he doesn't pick it up in a little black bag so he probably isn't a dog owner.

I walk on. Probably influenced by what I have just witnessed I wonder how many other people are taking a dump at this very moment. Must be millions. The population of the world is 7.5 billion; say just one per cent of them are having a dump at any one time, that's 75 million people having a dump right now. Say the average dump weighs a pound. That's 75 million pounds, or 33482 tons of shit. That's a lot of shit. How big would a 33482 tons pile of shit be? Would it be as big as, say, Ayers Rock? Probably. It would be roughly the same shape too if it had been dropped to the ground like the turd dropped by the man I had just seen having a dump. If you could somehow get it to Australia it could be another Ayers Rock, where it would add to the few things worth seeing there. They could have a new Ayers Rock every day: *'Come to Australia, forget the Great Barrier Reef and the Sydney Opera House, they're shit, come and see some real shit, our 1000 Ayers Rocks'.*

I stop for a while at one of several benches on the trail and scan the newspaper headlines. The front page reports on the terrible bombing at the Manchester Arena. Earlier, whilst in the newspaper shop, I heard on their radio a politician speaking about it, the platitudes slipping effortlessly from his mouth. *"Clearly we will not let this atrocity affect us; we will not let these maniacal terrorists rule our lives. We refuse to bend to their will. We will get on with our jobs as normal; we will go to our factories, we will go to our shops and our offices, we will go about our daily business as though it has never happened."* In the following news item it was announced that all General Election campaigns had been put on hold for a day as a token of respect. So everyone was going about their day as normal except for the politicians. Why am I not surprised? Only politicians.

On the inside pages of the paper a headline catches my eye. 'RADIO HOST'S 'GUESS THE LINK' TO MOORS KILLER. Apparently on BBC Radio Leeds yesterday listeners were asked by the show's host, one Nathan Turvey, to 'guess who it is' from the clues offered up by four songs he played. The answer was Moors Murderer Ian Brady. Amongst the songs were 'The Brady Bunch', The Smiths 'Suffer Little Children' and 'Psycho Killer' by Talking Heads. What a sad, sad world we live in. I hope this cretin was dragged outside, disembowelled, and his innards thrown to the crows.

I spot another interesting headline. 'GARDENING CAN CUT THE RISK OF CANCER'. It is today's 'Things you have to do if you want to live longer' article. There is at least one of these every day, if you can't find it you're not looking hard enough. Today's messianic message is to post-menopausal women, informing them that they could cut the risk of breast cancer by 13 per cent if they took up gardening. In my mind's eye I see the following being enacted in homes throughout the country. *"Oy, Deidre! Put that Chat magazine down and get your arse off the couch and into the back garden, there's a foot deep trench to be dug for my King Edwards."* The article goes on to say that post-menopausal women would further improve their chances of not getting breast cancer by a further 17 per cent by doing 'vigorous exercise such as running or fast cycling'. *"Oy, Deidre! Every so often put your spade down and do a swift turn round the garden on our Darren's mountain bike."* These breast cancer-countering measures would be diminished by 9 per cent, however, the article warns, if just one small glass of wine per day is consumed. So there's a choice then. Gardening, vigorous exercise, 30 per cent less chance of getting breast cancer. Gardening, vigorous exercise, small glass of wine a day, 21 per cent less chance of getting breast cancer. Or you can just say *"Bollocks to it, I'm having three glasses of wine a day - I might die earlier but at least I'll die happy and without being knackered from all that digging and riding a bike round the bloody garden."*

I continue my walk. Being a weekday there are few people about. No horses thank goodness. So no assault on my nostrils every time one or more pass by. If there is a God he isn't doing me any favours, otherwise why would a horse's anus be exactly the same height off the ground as my nose? (To counteract this problem I thought I might one day try walking along in a squat, the way Groucho Marx walks, but with my luck someone on a Shetland pony would ride past.) Soon, an unexpected cyclist whooshes past me from behind at about a hundred miles an hour. No warning from his bell of course. Ten to one on he hasn't got one. Why don't bikes have bells nowadays? I shout after him, asking him if he's trying to win the No Bell prize but I doubt he hears my query, and even if he does it probably goes over his head. I pass and swap 'hellos' with Arthur Gibb, who is the tightest man I have ever met. It is said, and Arthur has never denied it, that he has never taken advantage of a supermarket '3 for the price of 2' offer in case he dies after eating the first.

When I return home it's time for lunch. I always have two boiled eggs, a couple of crispbreads, an orange. After lunch I read the newspaper for half-an-hour or so with my cup of tea. I make my way back to the computer to do a further hour's writing. Maybe I will add to what I have already written earlier, more probably I will re-write it, often finishing with less than I started with. (Once, I remember searching my mind for the best part of an hour for the exact clause I needed to make a sentence perfect. The following day I discarded the entire sentence.) An old friend, the comedian and writer Barry Cryer, once told me that he could write with most people but John Cleese was not one of them. He and Cleese would write a sketch together and immediately they had finished Cleese would set about re-writing it. Then he would re-write it again. Then again. And again. He was never satisfied. It used to drive Barry mental. But perhaps it was all the re-writing that made Cleese such a brilliant writer? Word is that it took him six weeks to write each of the twelve episodes of the peerless *Fawlty Towers*. It showed. It doesn't make me a brilliant writer but I like to think my constant re-writing makes my stuff at least worth a read.

I finish writing for the day and do the *Telegraph* crossword puzzle. I do this not only because I have always enjoyed doing crosswords but also because I once read - probably in one of the *Telegraph's* 'Things you have to do if you want to live longer' articles, that doing crossword puzzles helps to keep the mind active and stave off the onset of Alzheimer's Disease and dementia. I do this not only because I have always enjoyed doing crosswords but also because I once read - probably in one of the *Telegraph's* 'Things you have to do if you want to live longer' articles, that doing crosswords helps to keep the mind active and stave off the onset of Alzheimer's Disease and dementia. I do this not only because I have always enjoyed doing crosswords but also....sorry, sorry. Now where was I? Ah yes.

I take another stroll along the Trail, this time in the opposite direction. What an exciting life I lead. When I get back I prepare and eat my evening meal. It has to be something nice. This is a meal for a man who has so far today only eaten fruit, yogurt, nuts, boiled eggs and crispbreads. Tonight it is a Gloucester Old Spot free range pork chop, home-made apple sauce, Jersey Royal potatoes tossed in butter and mint, asparagus, carrots finished in the juice of an orange and nutmeg. Fresh strawberries, raspberries and blueberries, full fat yogurt, honey to follow.

Lovely.

After I wash and dry the dishes I travel to Hazel Grove, about six miles distant, to play crown green bowling, my sport of choice nowadays. Bowls is a humble sport, the only kit you need in order to play it a set of bowls. You play in whatever clothes you feel comfortable in; there's no dressing up to be done as in most other sports, no adorning yourself to look like Rupert Bear to play your golf, no spending hundreds of pounds on whites, caps, helmets, bats, pads, boxes and other paraphernalia to play your cricket. I win my game, just, 21-19. Happy days.

On the way home, feeling a bit peckish, I call in at a Subway. Despite what I wrote about Subway in *Dear Pepsi-Cola*, where I made the point that my six inch sub was habitually less than six inches (by definition making the other half, bought by someone else, more than six inches), I quite enjoy a turkey and ham sub. I could do without Subways' taste in music though, which is invariably the radio tuned in to Radio One, a noise that does nothing to improve the atmosphere and probably contributes, over the course of the day, to the withering of the salad selection's lettuce. I arrive home at about ten, arm myself with a generous glass of wine (claret tonight, often burgundy or something from the Rhone valley), and watch part three of *The Trial*, something new I am following on TV. It ends at 11.30 p.m. I judge that the man accused of strangling his wife is not guilty. (On completion of the case, two days later, it is revealed that he is guilty. If I am ever picked for jury service the defendant won't know how lucky he is.) Tomorrow is a new day. It will start for me sometime between 12 midnight and 1.30 a.m.

Since writing the above two more 'Things you have to do if you want to live longer' articles appeared in the 7th of June edition of the Daily Telegraph. One, 'YOGA EASES PAIN OF BREAST CANCER PATIENTS' advised that women including yoga in their daily exercise routine will boost their energy and wellbeing. (Although it doesn't point out the dangers of doing this whilst riding a bike round the garden or digging a trench for the potatoes, which could be a bit tricky.) A second, 'DAILY GLASS OF WINE RAISES RISK OF ALZHEMER'S' is yet another warning about drinking to excess. However if a woman has taken the "Bollocks to it, I'm having three glasses of wine a day - I might die earlier but at least I'll die happy" option she will not only have the benefit of more energy but will also feel extra good about it. If, that is, the Alzheimers doesn't make her forget all about the various warnings and she carries on as usual.

****

May 28 2017. *ATKINS'S WOMAN.*

"I wish I'd never helped her in with her shopping," Atkins moaned, his face as long as a wet week in Wigan. "I wouldn't have if I hadn't noticed a two-pack of mangoes peeping out of the top of one of her shopping bags. Well you know me, I'm a martyr to mangoes; I was hoping she'd give me one for my trouble if I dropped a hint. Now I can't get rid of the bloody woman. And I didn't even get a mango."

She, is Mrs Pallister, recently widowed, sixtyish, who moved into Atkins's adjoining semi about a week ago.

"She's set her cap at me and no mistake. A bloody Valentine's Card arrived in the post this morning."

"I thought Valentine's Day was in February?"

"You see what I mean? She's ringing my doorbell every five minutes. It started with her lasagne. *"I've made too much lasagne, would you like the other half? It would be a shame to waste it."* Then it was a whole lasagne. *"Silly me, I've made too much lasagne again. I thought rather than bring your half round we might as well eat it together, well we're both on our own now, aren't we."* My bloody half! Then it was a lasagne and a bottle of wine. Christ knows what she'll turn up with next, probably a lasagne, a bottle of chianti and an Italian bloke playing the violin. Yesterday she told me two can live as cheaply as one. I can't keep her away, Razza, she was even on my doorstep tonight when I came round to see you. *"Have you got such a thing as a drop of milk you could let me have, Richard?"*

"Oh it's Richard by now, is it?"

"Yes it bloody is! Not at *my* invitation I can tell you. She asked me to call her Genevieve. She's got no chance. And stop grinning, this isn't funny."

"I'm sure she's only being friendly."

"Friendly? She wants more than friendly. The

other day she asked me to keep an eye on the weather. *"I'm off to do a spot of shopping, if it rains would you be ever so good enough to bring my washing in?"* If it rains! A blind man could see it was going to rain, the clouds were nearly touching the rooftops. You should have seen the contents of her washing line! There was nothing on it but knickers and bras and black stockings and suspender belts; and not just ordinary knickers and bras either, sexy knickers and bras."

"You brought them in for her then?"

"I felt like a bloody pervert."

A thought struck me. "Didn't you mention she told you she'd down-sized?"

"What's that got to do with it?"

"Well if she's down-sized she's got money. From the sale of the house she down-sized from. I would have thought that a man with your love of making money would have jumped at the chance of a liaison with a wealthy widow?"

"I don't want any more money; I like making money for the thrill of making money, not because I need it, I don't want it just handed to me. Besides, have you seen her?"

"She's not bad. I'm sure she has some attractions."

"Yes well one of them isn't a big pair of tits. And big tits are right at the top of my shopping list when it comes to women, as you well know. Anyway, even if she had a pair like Dolly Parton I don't want her ringing my bell anymore; I've had enough of it."

"You'll just have to put her off you then, won't

you."

"Well I know that don't I, but how?"

"I would have thought that just by being yourself would have put her off, but obviously it hasn't."

"Ha bloody ha. Come on, Razza, think, you have a friend in need here."

"Perhaps you could tell her you've got a venereal disease? Or better still, Aids."

"Aids? That's a bit extreme, isn't it?"

"It would put her off you."

"It would put everybody off me."

"Oh I don't know; the world is a lot more tolerant about people with Aids nowadays."

"I am not telling her I've got Aids!"

"All right, all right, keep your shirt on. Especially if Mrs Pallister is round at yours," I couldn't help adding with a smile

"It's not funny, Razza, I'm bloody desperate here. Please? Come on, you're the ideas man."

"I'm the 'stands a chance of succeeding' ideas man."

"So let's be having one then."

The following day I rang Atkins. "I've been having a think about your little problem and...."

"Big problem. Big, big problem."

"Big problem. And I think I may have the answer."

"Great. Go on then."

"You're going to have to demonstrate to her, in no uncertain terms, that she has not got a snowball's chance in hell of landing you."

"Right. How?"

"Patience, patience. Here's what I want you to do. Make arrangements for her to call round on you one night...."

"I can't *stop* her calling round. Usually with a bloody lasagne."

"So it won't be a problem then. She comes round, as arranged, only to find you on the sofa, if not *in flagrante* then very close to *in flagrante*, with a very attractive much younger woman. And before you ask me where this very attractive younger woman is coming from my daughter has agreed to play the role."

A delighted intake of breath came through the phone. "Has she? Your Carol-Ann?"

"My Carol-Ann."

"She's a doll," said Atkins appreciatively. "If Mrs Pallister sees me in.....what did you call it?"

"*In flagrante*."

"That's like getting the legover, isn't it?"

"Yes, but in this case seemingly *about* to get the legover."

"Well of course. I like your idea. I like it a lot."

"Can you fix it for tonight?"

"It's fixed."

Carol-Ann, in addition to sharing my sense of fun, shares the lovely looks of her mother, and also the good fortune, again like her mother, of looking much younger than her years. Although just the wrong side of fifty, she could easily pass for mid-thirties. I didn't see what she wore when she was with Atkins but she talked of a black basque and stockings she once wore when attending a performance of the *Rocky Horror Show*. The idea was for Atkins to ask Mrs Pallister round, leave the front door ajar, and when she rang the doorbell call out *"I'm busy in the lounge at the moment, come right in an join me."*

Soon after the appointed hour of the assignation Atkins was on the phone to me, ecstatic.

"It worked! Worked like a charm. Your Carol-Ann was magnificent, quite magnificent."

"Give me the highlights."

"There was only one. I called to Mrs Pallister to come in, she came in, she saw me on the sofa almost in what's-its-name with Carol-Ann, Mrs Pallister's chin nearly hit the floor, Carol-Ann turned to her with the most wonderful look of disdain and said *"Hoppit, Grandma"* and she hopped it. Never to return, with any luck. No, no luck about it, I'm sure it'll have seen her off for good. I can't thank you enough, mate."

"My pleasure."

The line went silent for a moment or two then Atkins said, "I'm thinking of asking her out."

"Mrs Pallister? I thought....?"

"No. Carol-Ann."

"What?"

"Carol-Ann. I'm thinking of asking her out."

I couldn't believe my ears. *"You're thinking of asking her out?"*

"Well, I mean we're both unattached, I'm a

widower and she's divorced, so I thought.... why not?"

"Why not? I'll tell you why bloody not. She's young enough to be your daughter. She *is* my daughter. That's why not."

There was a lengthy pause. And then Atkins, trying to redeem himself said, "It was only a thought."

"Well it's a thought you need to get out of that addled brain of yours, and bloody fast."

"Sorry. Sorry, I must have got carried away. But you can't wonder; it was really nice sat with my arm around her on the sofa. And those stocking tops....and it's a long time since I...."

"I don't want to hear this, Atkins."

"No. No of course you don't. Sorry."

"I should bloody well think you are too," I said, and slammed the phone down.

I won't let this come between Atkins and me but I shall be keeping a very close eye on him in future.

****

May 30 2017. *MEMORIES OF AN EIGHTY-YEAR-OLD NEXT BIRTHDAY - GROWING UP.*

I am seven years old. Dora, my Granny Ravenscroft, is sat in her rocking chair by the fireside, her permanent position during the day apart from an occasional trip to the front door *"To stretch me legs."* Whenever she does this my young mind wonders why, having stretched her legs, she is never any taller. I don't know how old Dora is, only that she is old, but at my age twenty is old. She is wearing a hair net, as permanent a feature on her head as was Ena Sharples's in years to come. Dora never says much, and then usually only to criticise: *"Have you seen t'state of her over t'road's curtains? I'd die o' shame if they were mine."*

Dora is my cash machine, I can always get a tanner (sixpenny piece) out of her. All I need do is tell her that my Grandad Smith, who also lives with us, and whom she hates, has given me a threepenny bit. In next to no time, with a look that says *'I'll show him if he'll give you threepence!'* she is into her purse. (This doesn't mean that I then have ninepence - Grandad Smith never gives me threepence, he doesn't like me. Dora told me it's because I'm good-looking and he's a frazzled ugly old bugger.)

Dora goes to the pictures (the cinema) every Wednesday, whatever the film, whatever the weather. She always has a seat booked for her - you could in those days - in row L. *"Get me a seat in 'ell,"* she says to whoever she is telling to book the seat. Her favourite films are those that have *"That bloody big dog."* (the MGM lion) at the beginning. Today, whilst rocking in her chair, she lets rip with an enormous fart. It is easily the loudest, ripest, fart I have ever heard. It smells even worse than it sounds, so pungent it probably adds to the colour of the whitewashed ceiling, already stained a dark tan from the nicotine of my mam's and dad's Woodbines and Park Drive. I have never heard Dora fart before. I never want to hear her fart again. I am the only other person in the room. After several seconds pass she turns to me and says: *"I don't fart very often, young Terry, but when I do it's a good 'un."* I never hear her fart again, but she dies a couple of months later. I don't think it has anything to do with the fart.

*

I am eight. At school, in Class 2, it is poetry, a one hour lesson we endure every week. Our form teacher is Miss Snotrag, known by this name ever since a fellow pupil, smarter than me, discovered that her real name, Gartons, was Snotrag spelt backwards. (We also have a Miss Twat, but her real name is Hargreaves; she is known as Miss Twat because she's a twat.) Miss Snotrag recites a poem to us from a thick book. I have heard it maybe fifty times before and am quite sure I will be hearing it again. It is learning by rote, memorisation by repetition. Most of what the poets are saying, in their limericks and sonnets and blank verse, goes way over our heads. Miss Snotrag never explains to us the things they are saying in different words, in metaphors, in similes, in allegories, so perhaps she doesn't know either. Learning by rote works for me with times tables - if asked what seven nines are I can say quick as a flash that they're sixty-three - but not for poetry. I could read *Paradise Lost* for the rest of my life and I still wouldn't have a clue what Milton is on about.

In the back of the book is an index of all the poems, in alphabetical order, along with the names of their author. All the great poets are represented; Shelley, Keats, Wordsworth, Coleridge. And the best of the lot, Longfellow, who penned *Hiawatha*, my favourite. Wordsworth can keep his daffodils, Coleridge can stuff his albatross, give me *Hiawatha* any day of the week - *'On the shores of Gitche Gumee!'* Longfellow's middle name was Wadsworth. I would love my middle name to be Wadsworth and have tried it on for size more than once: *Terence Wadsworth Ravenscroft*. But I don't even have an ordinary middle name, let alone one as grand as Wadsworth; people don't have middle names where I come from, and if you did have one you wouldn't dare telling anyone for fear of them making fun of you.

One poet in particular is represented in our poetry book many, many more times than the other poets, as much as all the other poets put together. To Coleridge and Shelley's four or five poems he is credited with eighty four. I've counted them. His name is Arthur Unknown. (On seeing Arthur's surname my eight-year-old brain, still nowhere near attuned to the many vagaries of English pronunciation, has pronounced it with a hard 'k', and the 'ow' sound as 'ou', thus in my head, fixed for all time, it is Arthur Unk-noun.)

Growing up, and in adulthood, I came across the names of Shelley, Keats and the other poets many times, but never Arthur Unknown. I wondered why. I asked people. *"John, you're well read, have you ever heard of a poet named Arthur Unk-noun?"* No one had. I was thirty-seven before it dawned on me. On first seeing Arthur Unknown's name in print I had read the word 'Author' as 'Arthur'. It was '*Author* Unknown' - the author of the poem was unknown! Did I feel stupid or did I feel stupid? I never told anyone, of course. Until now, when I'll be eighty next birthday.

*

I am twelve. We are having home-made steak and kidney pudding for tea (dinner to southerners). My mam (always mam, never mum or mother, this is the north of England) is a great cook of plain food and makes the best steak and kidney pudding in the world. It is quite wonderful, big chunks of skirt steak and kidney, rich gravy and thick suet pastry, 'feed me till I want no more' food. It later transpires that on making the pudding Mam couldn't find her 'steaming rag', the two feet square piece of muslin she wraps the pudding in prior to steaming it. The pudding was made, she had to use something, so in place of her steaming rag she used a pair of her knickers. (We are speaking here of a pair of 1950 women's knickers, a garment much more voluminous in those days; you couldn't steam a decent-sized dumpling in some of the knickers worn by the women of today.) No one would have known a thing about it if, after tea, my elder sister Monica hadn't seen the knickers in the kitchen, bits of suet pastry stuck to them, before Mam had chance to put them in the wash. It came out a couple of days later. *"Mam, when are we having knicker pudding again?"* said Monica, with a mischievous grin. *"You cheeky little bitch,"* said Mam. *"You tell a soul about what I steamed that pudding in and I'll swing for you!"* And clouted her one round the head as a reminder. Mam never made steak and kidney pudding again, despite my many pleas. More than likely it was because its appearance on the table would remind us that the last time it had been served up it had been steamed in a pair of her knickers. It would have dented her pride. She never said and we didn't dare ask. Whatever it was, I had eaten the last steak and kidney pudding she ever made.

*

I am fourteen. With me are schoolmates Skull (Alf Dawson), Bullneck (Skull's twin brother Bernard), Winner Binner Cow Curly Skunk (Jimmy Winch), Big Squeak (Alan Wheatcroft), Little Squeak (Big Squeak's younger brother Colin), Woodlouse (Walter Woodhouse), and Twig (Donald Fridlington). For some reason, I have no idea why, I am the only one of us, in fact the only boy I know, without a nickname. I would like a nickname, my preference being D'Artagnan, or, if I can somehow develop a hump, Quasimodo, but I don't push for one in case I end up with a nickname like two of my class mates, Slug and Shittyarse.

The eight of us are travelling home on the train from 'The Zoo' in Manchester, or to give it its full name, Belle Vue Zoological Gardens, a trip we make every Saturday night without fail. The attraction for us is not zoological, not the elephants or tigers or birds of prey, but even so an entertainment not lacking in the wildness of its participants - the free-style all-in wrestling at the King's Hall. We are of an age when we still half believe the terrifying things that Giant Anaconda and The Zebra Kid do to each other both in and out of the ring. (I once saw Jumping Jimmy Hussey live up to his name and jump up and down on the prostrate Wheelbarrow Watkins in the aisle by the sixth row).

On the train journey home, aping our wrestling heroes and stripped down to our underpants, we always re-enact the bouts that have thrilled us earlier, or at least start re-enacting them before getting carried away and adding bits of our own. Tonight I have already defeated Winner Binner Cow Curly Skunk two falls to one, ending the contest with an expertly executed Boston Crab in one of the string roof racks. The second bout of the evening was declared a double disqualification when Big Squeak illegally jabbed his elbow into Twig's face and Twig illegally bit it. The third encounter saw a grudge fight between Skull and his identical twin, Bullneck. Last week in school the headmaster had caned Bullneck in mistake for Skull and not only had Skull done nothing to try to prevent the punishment handed out to his sibling but had laughed in his face when Bullneck complained about it afterwards. Tonight, perhaps poetically, certainly justifiably, Bullneck had exacted revenge by knocking out Skull in the third round (although there was nothing poetic or justified about him kicking his brother in the ribs a couple of times after he'd knocked him out). Personally I thought this was a bit off colour, but everyone else seemed comfortable with it so I kept my mouth shut.

We are no more than a mile from home when the final contest, Woodlouse versus Little Squeak, gets underway. It must end by the time the train arrives at our station, New Mills Central, just as the Kings Hall's last bout must end by nine-o-clock to satisfy a local bye law set in stone. (One night, due to the third fight going on longer than it should have, it was two minutes to nine before the wrestlers entered the ring for the final bout. It ended at a minute to nine when, on shaking hands before the commencement of the fight, Man Mountain Dean held on to Jumping Jimmy Hussey's hand, took hold of his elbow in his other hand, raised his knee and brought Jumping Jimmy's forearm crashing down on it, causing Jumping Jimmy to howl in pain and jump higher than anyone had ever seen him jump before, and giving referee Dick the Dormouse no alternative but to disqualify him.)

Earlier Little Squeak had let it be known that all week, in anticipation of his fight tonight, he had been perfecting his drop kick, a wrestling move in which the wrestler launches himself into a horizontal position and kicks out his feet, the object being to knock out his opponent, or at least knock him through the ropes, by smashing into his face with the soles of his wrestling boots, or in Little Squeak's case the soles of his dad's clogs, specially 'borrowed' for the occasion. He now produces the clogs and puts them on. Woodlouse objects strongly to this but Little Squeak tells him not to be so bloody mard - just about the worst thing you can be accused of when you're a fourteen year old lad - and Woodlouse reluctantly lets it go.

The bout commences. After a cagey first minute in which the opponents warily stalk each, each waiting for the other to make the first move, Little Squeak never taking his eyes off Woodlouse's eyes, Woodlouse never taking his eyes off Little Squeak's clogs, Little Squeak suddenly launches his drop kick. Expecting it, having being pre-warned, Woodlouse ducks as

Little Squeak kicks out with his legs. Little Squeak's impetus carries him clean over Woodlouse. The two are right at the end of the carriage and if it hadn't been a warm night Little Squeak would have crashed into the door's glass window and probably cut himself badly. But it is a warm night and someone had previously wound down the window to let in some fresh air and instead of crashing into it Little Squeak soars clean through it and out into the pitch black of the night.

Winner Binner Cow Curly Skunk is the first to react. "Fuck me! He's gone!"

Twig is the second. "Quick, pull the communication cord!"

I am nearest to the communication cord. I quickly stand on the seat and make to pull it.

"Hang on, hang on," says Woodlouse, alarmed. "There's a twenty-five pound fine for improper use of the communication cord." He points at the notice. "See, it says there."

"Is stopping to pick up somebody who's jumped out of the window improper use?" asks Winner Binner Cow Curly Skunk, pragmatically.

"No it bloody well isn't," says Big Squeak.

"Yes well you would say that, you're his brother," says Skull, at the same time proving that being knocked out a few minutes ago hadn't done any damage to his powers of reasoning.

"Yes, so that means I've got to look out for him!" says Big Squeak.

"I don't think it's improper use either," says Twig.

"Well I bloody well *do*," says Skull.

"I think it is," says Winner Binner Cow Curly Skunk. "You aren't supposed to jump out of train windows, anybody knows that."

"Anyway it's all your fault, Woodlouse," says Big Squeak, changing tack. "If you hadn't ducked he wouldn't have gone through the window."

"So I'm just supposed to stand there while he kicks me with a pair of bloody clogs on, am I?"

"It wouldn't have hurt you much. He said you were a mard sod, now you're proving it."

"How much is that each, twenty five pounds?" says Bullneck, returning to the matter at hand.

I work it out. "Eight of us, including Little Squeak, about....three pounds four shillings."

"I don't give a monkey's doodah how much each it is, *I'm* not paying it," says Skull.

"I'm not paying it either," says Winner Binner Cow Curly Skunk, "I only get two quid for my paper round and I've got me fags to pay for out of that."

"Well I'm not paying if him and Skull aren't paying," says Woodlouse.

Big Squeak appeals to us. "We *have* to pull the communication cord." He gives good reason. "He's got me dad's clogs on, me dad'll kill him, they're his work clogs."

"He might already be dead. Or out there dying while we could be helping him." I say, in an appeal to the better nature of those who are against pulling it.

Twig hasn't got a better nature. "Well it's his own bloody fault for jumping out of the window."

"*And*, if he's already dead, that'll mean it'll be

more than three pound four shillings towards the fine, because there'll only be seven of us, it'll be four pound odd," says Woodlouse. "*I'm* not paying four pound odd for nobody,"

My own feelings are that we should pull the communication cord and sort out who pays for it later, if we have to. So, and although fearful of the consequences, I pull it. With a loud screeching of brakes and a lot of clanking noises the train judders to a stop. Bullneck puts his head out of the window. He is amazed. "We're only about fifty yards from the bloody station!"

"I'm *definitely* not paying towards any fine," says Skull. "They're sure to fine us if we're only fifty yards from the station."

The train guard arrives. We tell him what's happened. He sends for the police. Half-an hour later a policeman arrives and questions us. He takes all our names and addresses - with a fine in the back of our minds we all give false ones, I am Laurence Wadsworth Hibbert of 23 High Street, Glossop - then tells us he's going to organise a search party to look for Little Squeak and that we should all make our way home. We're just about to set off when Little Squeak suddenly appears from down the line. There's nothing wrong with him, no cuts or anything, he isn't even limping. He tells us he rolled down the embankment and landed in a field, the long grass must have cushioned his fall. Skull asks him what took him so long if there's nothing wrong with him. Little Squeak says he lost one of his clogs and he spent a lot of time looking for it but couldn't find it. Big Squeak says his dad will fucking kill him.

*

I am fifteen. Three days into my first job. I have left school with no qualifications; mine was a secondary modern school, its pupils not encouraged to sit GCE exams as is the case at the grammar school. I can't think I would have passed many, maybe English and Maths at 'O' level, certainly Bunking Off at 'A' level - my record of non-attendance at Religious Instruction class alone would have guaranteed that. So I have become factory fodder. (When the careers master, or what passed for a careers master in those days - in my case it was the geography teacher but I think they took it in turns - asked me what I wanted to do when I left school I told him I wanted to be a footballer. He told me not to be so bloody silly. He wouldn't tell me I was being bloody silly now.) I am working in a bleach works. My job, along with about ten other boys of up to seventeen years of age, is to be lowered daily into a 'keir', which I can only describe as like a huge iron cauldron about fifteen feet deep by twelve feet wide. In the keir, in company with another boy, Reg, I am distributing a continuous 'rope' of unbleached woven cotton as it descends from above via a wooden winch. Taking it in turns, as our arms soon get tired, one of us deals with the rope of cotton whilst the other treads it down so as to get as much of it into the keir as possible. (As the pair of you walk around evenly distributing the rope you gradually work your way up until about four hours later it is full and the lid fitted, ready for the cotton to be boiled and bleached white. On first being lowered into a keir it went through my mind that we have progressed little since we were sending boys of my age up chimneys.)

It is a tradition that all new boys are 'oiled', i.e. their private parts are ceremoniously subjected to the contents of an oilcan after their trousers have unceremoniously been taken down by the other boys. Today, when Reg and me are about eight feet from the top of the keir, a head appears above us. It belongs to Ray Walker, the under-foreman, a man of about thirty, a bully. He bares his gums in a sneer and says to Reg: *"Has this little twat been oiled yet?"* Reg shakes his head and grins. He bears me no malice, he has been oiled himself, why shouldn't I be oiled too? It's what happens. *"Then he bloody well soon will be,"* says Walker, and with that reaches down, grabs hold of my hair and hauls me, screaming and struggling, out of the keir. Soon, I am oiled. I vow that one day, when I am fully grown and better able to take care of myself, I will get my own back on Walker.

After leaving the bleach works at eighteen to do National Service our paths don't cross until almost forty years have gone by. I am playing bowls for my club; Walker has come along with the opposing team as a spectator. I am fifty-three, not far past my prime. Walker is about seventy, smaller than me now, wizened with age. On seeing him my mind instantly goes back to the time he hauled me by the hair from the keir. But that was a long time ago. Received wisdom is that people who have sworn to 'get' somebody sometime in the future rarely do, and I was never one to bear grudges. I approach Walker. I smile. "Hello, Ray." He looks at me. Doesn't know me from Adam. I tell him. *"Terry Ravenscroft."* I hold out my hand for a handshake. He offers his. I pull my hand away, grab his hair and pull it as hard as I can. He squeals in agony, as I did.

*

I am sixteen. Along with a couple of mates from my junior football team, High Lea Athletic, I have been 'spotted' by a scout and selected for every young footballer's dream, a trial with a professional team. My dream is especially good as the trial is with Manchester United, '*The Red Devils*', my favourite team, the only team.

There are about forty of us assembled at United's training ground, The Cliff, Lower Broughton, all lads aged from fourteen to sixteen. The man in charge is wearing a black eye patch, has a mess of greasy-looking red hair down to his shoulders and wears a track suit that looks as if it has been a stranger to the washing basket for the last two years. I don't think it is Matt Busby. In a wheezy voice - probably caused by an-ever present fag dangling from the corner of his mouth - he tells us his name is Roy, to 'watch ourselves', whatever that means, and instructs us to kit ourselves out in a shirt from the two piles of shirts, one red, one blue, beside the touchline. Naturally, imagining ourselves as current United stars Jack Rowley and Stan Pearson - well I do - we all make a dive for the red shirts. Fortunately I manage to grab one. Unfortunately it is a shirt that seems to have been made for a man about ten feet tall and built like a brick shithouse. I'm still quite small for my age and when I put it on it almost brushes the turf. I point this out to Roy and he tells me to try to avoid brushing away the whitewash touchlines and to watch myself. I like to wear my football shirt outside my shorts like the current United winger Johnny Berry but dressed in the shirt I've ended up with it makes me look like an idiot so I tuck it into my shorts. There's so much to tuck in I look like the fat kid they always stick in goals so I quickly pull it back out again in case Roy gets it into his head I'm a goalie and puts me in goal.

Twenty two of us are formed into two teams and the game begins. I am one of those not playing but I'm not overly concerned; Roy has told us we will all get our chance, *if we watch ourselves.* I am sure he is looking at me when he says this. After about fifteen minutes Roy blows a long blast on his whistle to bring the game to a halt, calls about half the players off the pitch and tells some of us to take their places. I am one of the lucky ones. Roy tells me to play left back. "I'm a centre-forward," I quickly point out.

"Left back," he says and points to the left back position in case I don't know where it is. He is almost right; I've never played left back in my life. "I'm not a left back," I say. "I'm a tricky centre-forward. I'm very quick."

"Then you'll have no trouble finding your way very quickly to left back."

"But I'm a...."

"Left back!"

"But I'm a *centre-forward.*"

"A good footballer can play anywhere."

I persist. "I'll be wasted at left back, if you put me at left back I won't be able to demonstrate my deft dribbling and sharp shooting skills."

Roy looks at me as though he could kill me.

"LEFT BLOODY BACK!"

Meekly, shoulders slumped, I walk onto the pitch and take up position at left back. A minute later the Blues right winger skins me and scores a goal. He doesn't skin me again but only because I'm on the pitch for about another five minutes and the ball doesn't come near me again. I complain to Roy. "I was only on about five minutes; I didn't get the chance to demonstrate my dribbling and shooting."

"You'll get another chance later in the game. *If you watch yourself*," he says. I have to accept this, and watch myself.

Two more wholesale changes of players take place and a half-hour passes before I get another chance. The lad playing centre-forward for the Reds is rubbish, nowhere near as good as me. Just wait till I get on, I'll show everybody what a centre-forward is! Roy beckons me with a crooked finger. "You. On the field. Right back."

I can't believe it. "Right back?"

He fixes me with a baleful stare. "Are you deaf, lad, as well as daft? Right back!"

I fight my corner. "If I play right back I won't get chance to show you my dribbling and shooting skills!"

At this he takes a threatening step towards me and looks as if he's going to kill me again so in an effort to stop this happening, and also to pre-empt his next words, I say, "All right, all right, RIGHT BLOODY BACK!" and troop onto the field, even more unhappily than before, and take up position at right back.

On the way I develop a plan. The minute I get

the ball off the lad on the Blues left wing - and I am definitely going to get it even if I have to trip him up to get it - I'm going to burst forward towards the Blues goal. In my head I see myself cutting through the opposition like a knife through butter. I am a will o' the wisp, twisting this way and that, brushing aside tackles with a haughty disdain. It's as though the ball is tied to my boot, just as it will seem to be tied to Georgie Best's boot in years to come. From about twenty-five yards out, after leaving four of the opposition on their arses and scratching their heads in utter bemusement, I release a thunderbolt of a shot. The ball zooms like a tracer bullet into the top right hand corner of the goalposts. It breaks the net. The goalkeeper, rooted to the spot, can only watch it in open-mouthed awe. Old Trafford erupts. *"Terry Ravenscroft, Terry Ravenscroft, There's only one Terry Ravenscroft! Don't be soft, give the ball to Ravenscroft!"* There is little doubt in my mind that something very similar is now about to take place. And once Roy has seen my deft dribbling and dynamic finishing he will take me off the pitch immediately, wrap me in cotton wool and it will be first stop Matt Busby's office. United will sign me. *"No, thank you all the same Mr Busby but I'll have to say no to a glass of champagne, I have to keep myself fit and alcohol might be the ruin of me, I can't allow that happen."*

I don't even have to trip anyone up to get the ball. Our right half tackles their inside left and it lands at my feet, a gift from the Gods. I get it under control immediately and hare off down the pitch. With consummate ease and a snake-like wiggle of my hips I leave the first Blues player in my path for dead. Only to be flattened with consummate ease and an elbow in the ribs by the second Blues player in my path. Gasping for breath I get to my feet clutching my side in agony. Roy signals for me to come off. After I get my breath back and have assured myself that I haven't got any broken ribs I ask Roy if I'm going to get on again. He doesn't answer but his face tells me it will be over his dead body. I wonder if Stockport County would be interested in me.

*

I am seventeen. I am on my way to Blackpool with the youth club. (I will have cause to be grateful to Blackpool one day, but today, sadly, is not that day.) My friend Alan is sat alongside me. In the seat in front sit Celia and her friend Marjorie. The expression 'drop dead gorgeous' has yet to be been coined but if it had it would describe Celia perfectly. I have had my eye on her for ages. Now, both my eyes are fixed firmly on the back of her head, on her long dark brown ponytail and slim pale neck. Shall I give her ponytail a friendly little tug? Better not, she might not like it. Don't want to ruin my chances. Occasionally, when turning her head to speak to either Marjorie or one of the girls seated across the aisle from her, I get a glimpse of her profile. Celia hasn't got a best side, both sides are her best side, both are absolutely beautiful; big, brown, almost black eyes, skin as smooth as porcelain. I am a sucker for beauty (I still am); beautiful girls, beautiful countryside, beautiful cars, beautiful minds.

On arriving at Blackpool the boys and girls go their separate ways. I only see Celia once, briefly and at a distance, on the Pleasure Beach. I have visions of sharing a carriage with her in the dark of the Ghost Train, hugging her protectively when she screams and holds on to me, but she's out of sight before I can get anywhere near her.

Coming back on the coach there is much seat swapping as lads make their move on girls. I suggest to Celia that she and Marjorie do the same with Alan and me. (I have to steel myself to do this, it is a bold move for me - I never make advances so as to avoid the red-faced embarrassment I would feel should I be knocked back. It's silly, I know, but I am what I am.) Celia doesn't say yes but she doesn't have to, her smile says it. I am on cloud nine. Within five minutes, with my arm around her, I am on cloud ten. It is wonderful. She is wearing a black jumper; round her neck is a necklace with a crucifix. I hope she isn't thinking of becoming a nun. Below she is wearing a white pencil skirt. When she is standing, the skirt, I have noted with greedy eyes, is just above knee-length, the current fashion. Seated, it is much less than knee length, and although not thigh length displays enough of her lovely legs to get me excited. I was excited even before I sat with her. I promise myself that later, now I'm 'in' with her, I will ask if I can see her again.

When the coach arrives back at the youth club I walk Celia home. She lives on a farm; it is an uphill walk there, about a mile. I cherish every step of the way. About fifty yards from her home she suddenly stops and turns to me, her back to the low stone wall bordering her dad's farm. I see this is a signal, take her in my arms and kiss her.

After the kiss she looks at me and says, "Now kiss me properly." I wind myself up and kiss her as hard, as passionately, as I can. Breaking off the kiss I say, "How's that?" I expect her to say 'better' or 'wonderful' or perhaps, unable to find words for the thrill I have given her, I will just hear a contented "Hmmmmm" as she melts weak-kneed in my arms. But she says nothing. Instead she just looks at me with a blank, uncomprehending expression, shakes her head in disbelief and walks away. Surprised, bemused, I call after her, "Can I see you again, Celia?" "No," she says, irrevocably, over her shoulder.

It dawns on me the following day. By asking me to kiss her properly she meant she wanted me to go further. I hadn't because it was our first 'date' and you didn't try anything on your first date if you had any respect for the girl. You left it until the second date, or even the third if you really fancied her and didn't want to risk killing the goose that one day might lay the golden egg. But *"Kiss me properly"* had to mean something, and clearly it was more than a kiss. Maybe she wanted me to fondle her breasts through her jumper? Maybe she wanted me to fondle her breasts *under* her jumper, even under her *bra*! Maybe she wanted me to slip my hand up her pencil skirt and feel her up! Maybe....maybe it was the Holy Grail itself! Maybe she wanted me to shag her! But it is too late now. The chance has gone. Shit!

*

I am eighteen. I am in the Army, doing National Service at Hillsea Barracks, Portsmouth, four weeks into basic training. My squad, twenty of us, are standing naked in Indian file in the medical centre. An army doctor is giving us some sort of examination; I won't know what for or why until it's my turn to be examined, but someone has already looked up my bottom with a torch so it can't be that. In front of me in the queue is Alexander-but-everybody-calls-me-Sandy. I don't like him, he is boastful and has a big mouth. He turns to me. He looks at my groin, grins and scoffs, "Is that all you've got?" What I have got is pretty average from what I have seen of other penises in changing rooms and public lavatories. I look at Alexander-but-everybody-calls-me-Sandy's groin. His penis isn't pretty average, it is big, as big as his mouth, which is very big. I say nothing. The following week our squad commander, Corporal Ross, announces that on Sunday, which is supposed to be our day off, it will be 'A' Company's sports day, and that everyone has to take part in at least one event or go on sick parade and if they do go on sick parade they'd better have a bloody good reason. Alexander-but-everybody-calls-me-Sandy announces that he will be entering the 440 yards sprint, he's a cert to win it, it will be a cinch, he can run like the clappers, nobody else should bother entering. I put my name down for the 440. Sunday dawns, sports day begins. The 440 yards comes round. Alexander-but-everybody-calls-me-Sandy takes an early lead. I let him. At school, aged fifteen, I was the North West Derbyshire champion at 220 and 440 yards. After about two hundred yards I cruise past him. At about three fifty I stop and turn. Alexander-but-everybody-calls-me-Sandy is lying second but thirty yards adrift of me. I wait for him to catch up. When he does I say, "Is that all you've got?" Having said it I run on and win easily.

****

May 31 2017. *HOLE IN THE ROAD.*

Atkins's house, the last house in our row of semis, looks out onto a main road. The other day two road workers arrived, along with their customary tarpaulin-covered portable cabin - as necessary for their survival, it seems, as is the shell to a tortoise - and commenced to dig a hole at the side of the road. As usual when men are digging holes in roads the event immediately attracted a small but constantly changing audience. Atkins, seated in a deckchair in his front garden taking advantage of the pleasant weather, and being the observant chap he is, took note of this. He also noticed that at twelve noon precisely the men downed tools, removed their high visibility safety vests and hard hats, and disappeared down the road, to return some sixty minutes later. Atkins made it his business to see if the same thing happened the following day and at the same time. It did, and soon afterwards he was round at my house with an idea for another of our daft games. It wasn't likely to be a daft game we would be able to play very often, such as our 'Blind Men', but seemed well worth the effort for all that. Even so I was guarded. "There are always people taking an interest, are there?" I said. "There's no point in doing it if we don't have an audience; I don't want to be wasting my time doing unnecessary manual work, not with my back."

Atkins was adamant. "There's always at least a couple of spectators once they're in the hole. I've seen as many as six. They don't stop for long, admittedly, ten minutes or so at the most; but even if there's nobody there when we start there soon will be, I'd put my life on it."

This was reasonable. "Right. We'll do it."

What we did, today, when the workmen disappeared for their lunch break, was to don their vests and hard hats and take their places. After discouraging Atkins from using the pneumatic drill, which he had 'always wanted to have a go with', on the grounds that it would probably shake his false teeth out, we armed ourselves with shovels and got into the hole - it was only about a foot deep, but then the workmen had only been digging it for two and a half days. Thus ensconced, we proceeded to put on a realistic enactment of workmen digging a hole, alternating between doing a bit of digging and a lot of passing the time of day whilst leaning on our shovels. A man and his wife, he with a dog, she with an Aldi shopping bag, were the first to stop to watch us at our labours, soon to be joined by a man pushing a bike with a flat tire. At that point I laid down my shovel, climbed out of the hole, removed my hard hat, upturned it, surreptitiously slipped a few coins in it, went to the man with the dog, held out the hat and looked at him meaningfully.

"What?" he said.

I shook the hat. Coins jingled, an invitation to more coins to join them. "Collection."

"Collection? What for?"

"The entertainment."

"What entertainment?"

I indicated Atkins, still digging away industriously. "Me and my mate digging up the road."

The man scoffed. "Huh. That isn't entertainment."

"Well it's entertaining you. And you two," I said to the others. "Besides, the digging is only the start of the show we have for you today. For now it is cabaret time. Featuring a top comic, me, followed by a musical turn from Mr Atkins there, a baritone of some renown. But first, me." I went into my act, which comprised bits from old scripts I'd written years ago for Les Dawson which I'd cobbled together the night before. "Good day, ladies and gentlemen. Allow me to introduce myself. Ronnie Rednose, comedian extraordinaire. Let me first tell you a little about myself. I was born many years ago not many miles from here, in Stockport's Stepping Hill Hospital, known locally, and not without good reason, as step in ill, carried out dead. (This got a laugh from the man with the bike, who probably had grim experience of that hospital.) My mother had a particularly long and difficult delivery, largely because she'd forgotten to take off her tights. When I finally popped out the nurses thought I had two short white legs and two long brown ones. (This drew laughs from all three of my audience.) The Rednoses decided to share equally the responsibility of bringing up their son - however I proved to be a difficult baby, often throwing tantrums and crying for long spells, especially when it was my father's day to breast feed me. (More laughs, especially from the woman.) My parents were so poor they couldn't afford clothes for me so I had to stay in all the time. Then when I was three they bought me a hat so I could look out of the window. At the age of five I began my education. I was a bright child at school as my mother had painted my head with luminous paint so she could pick me out easily when she came to collect me. (This got a very big laugh, and now my audience, drawn by the laughter, was joined by two more passers-by.) A clever if highly strung boy I passed my eleven-plus at the age of nine, passed three GCE's at the age of eleven, and passed water in bed until the age of fourteen. (Very big laughs and applause.) Due to the latter, plus a south-facing window and the central heating being on full all the time, there was usually a rainbow in my bedroom. This gave me an early interest in meteorology. To find out more about the subject I visited the local library and asked if they had a book on it but unfortunately the librarian thought I said 'metallurgy' and I spent the next two years thinking that an iron bar was an isobar. Well that's all for the moment folks, but I'll be back later, after the stripper, with much more of the same. Thank you." I gave a little bow. The audience, now numbering eight, applauded enthusiastically. There was even a sort of rebel yell such as you get from the morons in the audience of *Strictly Come Dancing* and *Britain's Got Talent*. "But for now," I continued, "would you please welcome to the stage, with songs from the shows, your favourite and mine, Mr Richard 'Oklahoma' Atkins!" I led the applause before disappearing into the portable cabin to chat up the stripper. Meanwhile Atkins climbed out of the hole and took centre stage.

"Thank you, thank you, thank you, ladies and gentlemen," said Atkins graciously. "My first song this fine afternoon will be the great Slim Whitman's yodelling version of the song Indian Love Call, from the 1924 Broadway hit *Rose-Marie*." Hands clasped together, Atkins struck a pose and began to sing and yodel at the top of his voice.

When I'm calling you, Oo-Oo-Oo, Oo-Oo Oo-Oo Oo-Oo Oo
Will you answer too? Oo-Oo-Oo, Oo-Oo Oo-Oo Oo-Oo Oo.
That means I offer my life to you, to be my own
If you refuse me I will be blue, waiting all alone...."

And that was as far as he got. Let me say right now I'd be the first to admit that Atkins wasn't sitting in the front row when singing voices were handed out; even so I thought it was a bit premature of the audience, if not unforgiving of them, and notwithstanding my suspicion that Atkins had been joined in the second *Oo-Oo-Oo, Oo-Oo Oo-Oo Oo-Oo Oo* by a neighbourhood cat, for someone in the audience to shout out raucously: "Bring back the comic!" Which was quickly followed by a shout of: "Yeh, you're rubbish you, bring the funny feller back!" I quickly emerged from the cabin to hear chants from the entire audience of "We want the comic, we want the comic!" I could see that Atkins, who has a Welshman's opinion of his singing prowess, i.e. it is nowhere near as good as he thinks it is, was not best pleased. His back up, he glared at the audience. "What's bloody wrong with my singing?"

"How long have you got?" said a tall man who looked as though he could handle himself.

"You cheeky bastard," said Atkins, rolling up his sleeves and making for the man. I am sure I have mentioned before that Atkins can be quite uncompromising when he thinks he has been slighted and the tall man's comment had made him feel very slighted. Aware of the likely outcome I rushed forward before there was blood and managed to get my body between the two.

"Leave it!" I said to Atkins, wrapping my arms around him. Despite his protests I bundled him towards the hole and managed to persuade him that our best course of action was to get back in the hole and take up our shovels. Thankfully he saw sense, and this is what we did. The audience, on seeing that more shovelling and leaning on our shovels passing the time of day was the only further entertainment they were going to get, began to drift away. The man with the bike asked when the stripper was coming on but I ignored him. When they had all gone we put the hard hats and vests back and cleared off before anyone else stopped to watch us.

I gave our daft game eight out of ten. Atkins, miffed that his singing hadn't gone down too well, only a six. We will think twice about playing it again, if the opportunity ever arises.

****

June 1 2017. *ROLF HARRIS.*

Dateline 1st June 2017, Derby Crown Court.

JUDGE: "Terence Ravenscroft. You are charged with the following offences. That on the thirty-first day of March, whilst walking through the outskirts of the village of Wardlow in the County of Derbyshire, you came across a sign saying 'CAR DRIVERS! STRICTLY NO TURNING!' by the entrance to the drive of a house. Considering that this was petty and mean-spirited, as car drivers would have to drive a considerable distance on the surrounding countryside's narrow lanes before finding a place wide enough to turn, you took it upon yourself to pick up a fragment of the local limestone and chalk in the driveway the words 'DON'T BE SUCH AN ARSEHOLE'. Furthermore, that on the eighth of April, when stopped in your motor car by a policeman and asked to provide a sample, you removed his helmet and urinated in it. Furthermore, that on the fourteenth of April in the Whaley Bridge branch of Tesco you ran up and down the cooked meats aisle with your private parts hanging out shouting *"Ladies, don't miss today's special offer!"* Finally, that on the third of May on the inter-city train between Manchester and London you attempted to stuff the mobile phone of a sales area manager sideways up his rectum. How do you plead to these charges, guilty or not guilty?"

COUNSEL FOR THE DEFENCE: "My client pleads not guilty to all the charges, M'Lud, on the grounds that he could not remember any of the events in question."

An unlikely outcome to the charges levelled against me? Think again.

Dateline 31st May 2017, Southwark Crown Court, London.

Following the collapse of the case against him the entertainer Rolf Harris, 87, was yesterday cleared of indecently assaulting a 14 year-old girl after she asked him for an autograph at a music event for children in London. He was also cleared of twice groping another teenage girl and telling her she was '*a little bit irresistible*', and touching another complainant after a recording of the BBC children's show *Saturday Superstore* before asking her '*do you often get molested on a Saturday morning?*' Harris, who denied all the charges, did not give evidence, his lawyer saying that he did not remember any of the events in question.

The prosecuting counsel couldn't have been much good. I would have made a much better job of it: "Ladies and gentlemen of the jury, we are speaking here of a man who sings about tying kangaroos down, who enthuses lyrically about two little boys, who not only talks often of his didgeridoo but often plays with it in public, and I am sure we all know what the 'extra leg' referred to by Harris in his song 'I'm Jake the Peg with the extra leg' refers to. And we are asked to believe that this wretch of a man is innocent of the charges brought against him?"

The above is taken, more or less verbatim, from a newspaper article. It went on to say that Harris said, after being found not guilty of the charges after the jury had failed to reach a verdict, "I'm 87 years old, my wife is in ill health and we simply want to spend our remaining time together in peace."

I hope when he dies he rests in piss.

****

June 8 2017. *AN ATTACK OF POLITICAL CORRECTNESS.*

It was a news item on the radio about the pantomime *Snow White and the Seven Dwarves* that made me realise I had for some unaccountable reason become politically correct. Apparently one of those people who go about getting all upset on behalf of other people had said that *Snow White and the Seven Dwarves* should be banned as it was demeaning to dwarves. Normally I would have laughed at this, and maybe it would have passed through my mind that if the authorities were daft enough to actually do this the first people to complain would be dwarves, since *Snow White and the Seven Dwarves* offers up employment to quite a few of them every year for a few weeks either side of Christmas. But for some reason I didn't do that. Instead, to my great surprise, I found myself agreeing with the complainer. Considering it, I thought that rather than ban the pantomime altogether, an action that would be no help at all to people of restricted growth - I noted that already I had stopped using the word 'dwarf' to describe the dwarf population - that it would perhaps be a good idea to make it more inclusive and re-name it *Snow White and the Seven People of No Particular Size*, or, even more politically correct, *Snow White and the Seven People of No Particular Size, Some of Whom Should be Female, and Maybe a Couple of them Disabled*. There would be no Dopey in it of course, on the grounds that being called Dopey might, heaven forbid, hurt his or her feelings. And Grumpy would have to go too if only to do away with people saying *"Snow White woke up feeling Grumpy"* and upsetting grumpy people. I wasn't too happy about the name Snow White either. Perhaps, on alternate days, the panto could be called *Coal Black and the Seven People of No Particular Size, Some of Whom Should be Female and Maybe a Couple of them Disabled*? All the matinee performances would be called *Person of Mixed Race and the Seven People of No Particular Size, Some of Whom Should be Female and Maybe a Couple of them Disabled*.

After breakfast, when I started up my computer to continue putting this book together, political correctness really got a grip of me on re-reading the last thing I had written the day before. It was the opening to an amusing piece (I hoped) about my crown green bowling club. One of the teams I play for is the Veterans, which comprises of players aged sixty and over. We have just the one team. In my sick and politically incorrect mind I had dreamed up a fixture for another, fictitious team of veterans, which I planned to pin up on the notice board alongside our normal fixture, the idea being that the names of the players would be a pointer to the physical condition that old age has wreaked on many veteran bowlers, myself included. My hope was that it would raise a few laughs, albeit wry ones. The details were:-

'B' TEAM VERSUS CROMFORD CROCKS, AWAY.
(With the fairies)

Al Zeimers
Art Trubble
Joe Ill
D Mentia
Arthur Itis
Dai Beaters
V Harry Cosveins
Fred Dead

Reserves

Won Lung
N Large-Prostate

On reading it back to myself I cringed and gasped out loud. I couldn't believe what I had written! What on earth was I thinking of, making fun of people's illnesses? Utterly ashamed, I consigned it to the recycle bin without delay, dismissed it from my mind for evermore and started writing a piece about how wonderful it was to be old and how much I was looking forward to being pushed around in a wheelchair and having carers calling in on me several times a day to feed me and wash my private parts.

I brought to mind some things, previously A-OK, that have since been deemed politically incorrect: dodgem cars that now have to dodge other cars, on grounds of health and safety, rather than bumping into them; golliwogs on Robertson's Jam labels being no longer acceptable in case they upset black people; some Domino's Pizza branches no longer serving pizza topped with pepperoni, sausage or ham as it might offend Muslims; the children's book character Peppa Pig having to be redrawn because it wasn't wearing a seat belt when driving a car (I don't think the Muslims are all that keen on Peppa being a pig, either); a Norfolk recruitment boss being told by her local Jobcentre Plus that she couldn't advertise for 'reliable and hard-working' applicants because it might 'discriminate against the unreliable'; seaside Punch & Judy shows being banned because they are violent towards women; the word 'Brainstorming' being banned and replaced with 'Thought Showers' because it might offend epileptics. Previously I had laughed out loud at such examples of political correctness gone mad; now I found myself agreeing with those who had pointed out their offensiveness.

I went out for a walk, to ponder on my new point of view in regard to PC. I picked up my newspaper. At a bench I paused to read awhile. Inside was an item of news concerning former tennis star Martina Navratilova and how she had been critical of fellow ex-Wimbledon champion Margaret Court after the latter had claimed in a radio show that *'tennis was full of lesbians'*. Apparently Navratilova had claimed that Court was *'a racist and a homophobe'* because of this. It occurred to me that to appease Martina the venue should in future be known as the Martina Navratilova Hairy Armpits Arena. At the same moment I looked up as a passing woman caught my eye. She was wearing a pair of 'couldn't be arsed to get dressed properly' track suit bottoms and a skimpy top that might have been skimpy if it hadn't had about three stones of excess flesh packed into it. As she waddled along she was stuffing a large cream cake into her mouth. In her other hand a giant Twix awaited the same fate. Silently I called her a great fat lump. *And immediately realised that my attack of political correctness had gone away*! I breathed a sigh of relief, and blessed my returned to sanity.

****

June 10 2017. *ATKINS 2*.

No doubt still flushed with success following the sale of Victoria Beckham's knickers Atkins was round at my house this morning in a state of excitement about another money-spinning idea. On the face of it, it seemed to be a much better proposition than his idea of acquiring a supply of David Beckham's used underpants for resale.

"It can't fail," he said. "It's my best idea yet."

"Which isn't saying a lot."

Atkins ignored my jibe and went on. "If you see the number or word '2' after the title of a film, would you go to watch it?"

"What's the film called?"

"It doesn't matter. Anything. Say it's called....er.... *Shitehawk 2*."

"Then definitely. In fact I would watch it if it was just called *Shitehawk*. Especially if it had an exclamation mark after it." I tried it out in that very deep voice used by the man on the telly advertising forthcoming films. "*Shitehawk!* Miss it at your peril!"

Atkins looked at me patiently. "All right it isn't called *Shitehawk 2*. It's called something else. Say it's called...." He took time to think up an appropriate title.

I helped him out. "*Desmond Tutu 2*."

"What?"

"*Desmond Tutu 2*, the follow up to *Desmond Tutu*."

"Are you taking the piss?"

"Subtitled *Desmond takes up Ballet*."

"Look just be sensible will you, this is serious. We'll say the film is called....*Grasslands 2*. What would you think?"

"I would probably think it was a follow-up to a previous film called *Grasslands*."

Atkins clapped his hands together triumphantly. "*Exactly*. A successful film, right; the follow-up to a successful film called *Grasslands*. Because if *Grasslands* hadn't been a success the film company wouldn't be throwing good money after bad, right?"

I saw the sense in this and nodded, but not encouragingly. "That seems reasonable." Atkins was encouraged enough without any help from me.

Atkins rubbed his hands together like a bookie spotting a man with a wad of money in each hand and a sign on his hat saying 'I AM A SUCKER'. "So here's my idea. Ready?" With a smile a mile wide he said, "You put a '2' after the title of the *first* film. For *Grasslands*, read *Grasslands 2*. Seeing it advertised people will think to themselves: '*Grasslands 2*? I don't remember a film called *Grasslands* but it must have been pretty good if they've made a sequel. I'll go and watch it. Take the family. Spend a fortune on popcorn and ice cream." He looked at me eagerly. "What do you think?"

Honestly, I thought it was a good idea. However I immediately saw a snag. "How are you going to sell it?"

"I'll simply approach a film company or a producer. I can see Quentin Tarantino going for it in a big way, or maybe Martin Scorsese."

"They're directors. Auteurs, actually."

"What's that?"

"Auteurs? Film directors who influence their films to such an extent that they rank as their author."

Atkins nodded approval. "That's even better. An auteur will be *really* keen on my idea. I'll try Tarantino."

"What if he doesn't go for it?"

"Then I'll go for Martin Scorsese."

"But you'll already have pitched it to

Tarantino. What's to stop him using it without paying you for it?"

Atkins hadn't thought of that. I mulled it over for a moment. "You'll need to get Tarantino to buy the idea before you let him in on it."

"Well obviously. How?"

"By making it sound like such a good idea that it's absolutely irresistible."

"Right."

" Let's try it out. I'll be Quentin Tarantino, you be you. Here's the scene. You have your idea in an envelope, you tell me you have this great idea, it's in the envelope, but before you give me the envelope you tell me you want a thousand pounds for it."

"I was thinking ten thousand."

"Whatever. Let's play it out. Really sell it to me."

"Right." Atkins composed himself, thought about it for a moment or two, then, fingering an imaginary envelope, went into his pitch. "Here, Mr Tarantino, in this envelope," he began, tapping the envelope a couple of times with the backs of his nails, "I have an idea that will make you millions of dollars. Here, in this envelope." He tapped the envelope again for effect. "Maybe my idea will make you a hundred million dollars. But that's the absolute bare minimum, it could be as much as a billion, it is such a great idea. It is a truly wonderful idea. It is bigger than the introduction of the talkies. Bigger than the introduction of technicolor. Bigger than the introduction of stereophonic sound. It will revolutionise your whole marketing strategy." He tapped the envelope a third time. "My idea. In this envelope. And all I am asking for my idea is ten thousand pounds. What do you say?"

"Fuck off."

"What?"

"Fuck off before I tear your lousy head off your motherfuckin' shoulders, reach inside the hole and rip out your asshole from the inside!"

Atkins looked aghast. "What....what are you doing?"

"Being Quentin Tarantino. I'm not being me, I'm not being nice, as verified by no less than three heart doctors, I'm being Quentin Tarantino, who must be a right little shit judging from his films. *Reservoir Dogs*? *Pulp Fiction*? He must be a *real* piece of work! No, I'm saying what Tarantino would say if you approached him with an idea like that."

Doubt clouded Atkins's features for the first time. "You reckon?"

"I reckon. Quentin Tarantino, matey, is a hard-boiled auteur. He would never go for it. He certainly wouldn't give you ten thousand pounds for it, sight unseen. He'd be far more likely to rip the envelope from your grasp, take out the idea and stuff the envelope down your throat. No, what you need, Atkins my boy, if you're ever going to sell your idea, is a soft- boiled auteur."

Atkins thought about this for a moment. "Martin Scorsese? Do you reckon he might be soft-boiled?"

"*Mean Streets*? *Taxi Driver*? *GoodFellas*?" I shook my head. "I wouldn't have thought so."

Atkins went off to look up producers and

auteurs likely to be soft-boiled. I don't think he'll find any. All movie producers and auteurs are hard-boiled. It goes, as they say, with the territory. But who knows?

This might not be over yet. There could be an Atkins 2 Two. Starring Desmond Tutu.

****

June 12 2017. *FREE PLASTIC BAGS.*

About a couple of years ago the Government, in an effort to limit the amount of discarded plastic bags littering our public areas, passed a law requiring supermarkets to charge 5 pence per bag for the bags they had previously made available to their customers free of charge. It proved to be an unqualified success, in fact the only Government initiative I can recall being a success, either unqualified or qualified. These days you see far fewer discarded bags polluting the streets, almost everyone choosing to save and re-use their bags for future trips to the supermarket, rather than having to fork out, say, 20 or 25 pence for new bags. It has been especially successful for me, in that it has continued to provide me with a free source of plastic bags. Anyone requiring the same has only to do the following.

Do your shopping. Check out at the self-service tills. Scan your shopping. Press 'Pay'. You will then be offered a choice of the number of bags you require, 'No bags, one bag, two bags, three bags, four bags, five bags'. Press 'No bags'. Then press 'Pay'. Then take one, two, three, four or five bags as required for your shopping. Personally I never need more than a couple.

When I posted the above helpful money-saving tip on Facebook, so that other people could have the advantage of free bags, quite a lot people were hostile, calling me a rogue and worse. I have, however, no qualms whatsoever about doing it. After all it wasn't me who was throwing away plastic shopping bags and littering the streets, forcing the Government to do something about it; I have never thrown away a plastic bag in my life, so why should I have to pay for them in order to encourage other people not to throw them away?

All was going well until whilst shopping this morning I experienced a minor blip in my system. After putting my bottle of milk and a canned tomato soup on the space provided for purchases, pressing 'No bag', paying, then taking a bag, a voice behind me said, in an outraged tone, "You put 'No bag'!"

I turned to see the owner of the outraged voice, a red-faced man, although whether the red face was his normal complexion or due to his outraged condition I wouldn't know. I regarded him coolly. "What?"

"You put 'No bag' and you've taken a bag."

I looked him up and down. "I don't see a uniform? Or an identifying Co-op logo on your clothing?"

"What?"

"Or perhaps you're the Plain Clothes Bag Thief Detective?"

The man sneered. "Very funny I'm sure," He

looked me up and down. "People like you are an absolute disgrace. It's as good as theft, that is. It *is* theft. What would happen if everyone behaved like you're behaving?"

"What would happen is that the world would be a tidier place," I said. "For having 'stolen' the bag I use it to put my paper and plastic household rubbish in, which I then deposit in the brown wheelie bin provided, rather than put it along with any other rubbish in the general rubbish bin, or throw it over the fence into next-door's back garden when they're out, like many people do. It is a course of action I feel I shouldn't have to pay for. So if everyone 'behaved like me' there wouldn't be any plastic bags littering the streets at all."

The man thought about this, then not to be outdone said, "You're still stealing."

"But with sufficient justification to salve any guilty conscience I might have," I said. Then I put my shopping in the bag and stepped aside.

I didn't leave, but lurked behind the man as he took my place at the till and processed his tin of corned beef and multi-pack of potato crisps. When he came to the number of bags required option he paused, looked surreptitiously over his shoulder to his left, then to his right, where he saw me watching him. Then he smirked at me and pressed 'one bag'. But whether or not he would have helped himself to a free bag if I hadn't been there I don't know. But my bet is that he would, and will certainly be doing so in future. As some people reading this will no doubt be doing.

****

June 14 2017. *PARKING*.

"Could I be of assistance, Madam? In the parking of your car?" Making a great show of tipping his cap Atkins approached the woman who had been making heavy weather of parking outside the shoe shop for the last couple of minutes. In addition to the cap - a British Rail porter's hat with the insignia removed (Oxfam) - Atkins was wearing his black funeral suit, black shoes and a black tie. And very smart he looked too.

"Would you mind, awfully?" said the woman, pleasantly surprised. "I'm afraid I've never quite got to grips with parking."

Which was the very reason Atkins and I were outside the shoe shop. We had picked the shop in particular as not only was it situated on one of the few streets nowadays which allow unrestricted and free parking but also because anyone hoping to park outside it was in all probability a woman, women owning about twenty times as many pairs of shoes as men and in consequence of this visiting shoe shops twenty times more often. We had arrived, in our separate cars, in good time before the shop opened, and had parked two yards apart directly outside the shop's entrance.

Our attendance had been prompted by a magazine article Atkins had read in a dentist's waiting room. The article made the brazen claim that it was a fallacy that women were worse parkers than men (it was written by a woman writer). Atkins knew better, as do I. At a confident guess I would say that more than nine men out of ten will reverse into a parking space that is, say, a distance of six feet greater than the length of their car. At an even more confident guess I would say less than one woman in ten will do likewise. Most of them will ignore the space altogether and drive on in search of a larger space. Some will attempt to drive into the space. All of them will fail, save for the drivers of 4 x 4s, who will only succeed by mounting the footpath, possibly killing a few pedestrians in the process. On telling me about the article Atkins remarked that a good living might be had by simply offering to park a woman's car for her in such circumstances. I concurred. We were off!

On our arrival Atkins took up position outside the shop. I stationed myself by the doorway, content to merely observe. We didn't have to wait long. On seeing the parking space several women slowed down but had then driven on, almost certainly on realising it wasn't as long as the runway at Manchester Airport and therefore not possible to drive into. One woman had stopped, tried to drive into it, but before Atkins could offer assistance had driven on in frustration.

Now, Atkins smiled and said, "Not at all, Madam, it will be my pleasure to park up for you, it is my purpose in life." With a languid arm he invited her to step out of the car. "If you would be so kind?"

He opened the door and clicked his heels together as the woman stepped out onto the pavement. Being Atkins I was surprised he didn't throw her a salute. "It will be three pounds," he said, holding out the palm of his hand.

"What?" said the woman in surprise.

"Three pounds," Atkins reiterated. "The fee for my services. As official car parker."

"I have to pay?"

"If you wish me to park your car."

"Only I thought, when you said....I got the impression it was free?"

Atkins gave a sad shake of the head. "I would love to do it for free, love to, but unfortunately I have to make a living." I could swear I heard violins in the background.

"Three pounds?" the woman questioned, not completely happy about it.

Atkins nodded uncompromisingly. "Look at it this way; it would cost you at least that much in the car park down the road and you'd have to walk back. Who knows how many bargains you might miss? I believe there's a beautiful pair of slingbacks on offer at half price, Jimmy Choo's I believe."

The loss of possible bargains seemed to make up the woman's mind for her. "Yes, all right then," she said, and reached inside her handbag for her purse.

And that should have been that. Atkins and I had satisfied ourselves, as if we needed to, that the vast majority of women can't park at the roadside, and that there was money to be made from doing it for them. But it was then that the devil got into me, as it sometimes does. Perhaps it was because I was still feeling a bit narked with Atkins for daring to have designs on my daughter and I saw it as a way of getting back at him. Without ado I sprung into action. Approaching them at pace I called to the woman, "I'll do it for two pounds."

She turned to me. "What?"

"What?" echoed Atkins, thrown at this sudden turn of events.

I gave him a wink unseen by the woman and said to her, "I'll park your car for two pounds."

Atkins, now anticipating there was more fun to be had, quickly slipped back into character. "Ignore him, Madam." He made a fist and shook it at me. "Clear off if you value your health, or you'll get some of this."

"I tell you what," I said to the woman. "Forget the two pounds; I'll do it for one pound fifty."

Atkins was outraged. "What? One pound fifty? You're cutting my throat here." He sliced the flat of his hand across his throat dramatically. "He's cutting my throat, Madam, tell him to skedaddle before I fetch him one."

"Well?" I said to the woman.

"Well he *is* the official car parker," she said, persuading herself she was doing the right thing.

"Yes, I *am* the official car parker," said Atkins.

I eyed him with contempt. "No you're not; you're no more the official car parker than I am."

"Oh no? Well if I'm not the official car parker why am I wearing an official car parker's uniform?"

"You aren't." I turned to the woman, "It's his funeral suit and a railway porter's cap."

Atkins was gobsmacked. "Wh....what?"

"And if you want further evidence that he is not a man to be trusted he recently tried to start an affair with my daughter behind my...."

Atkins jumped in. "I *thought* about starting an affair with your daughter!"

" ....tried to start an affair with my daughter behind my back."

"Did you?" said the woman accusingly, turning on Atkins.

"No. No of course I didn't. He's lying."

"I'll do it for a quid," I said. "Final offer."

The woman took a pound coin from her purse and gave it to me. With a withering look at Atkins she said, "You ought to be ashamed of yourself, a man of your age. I've a good mind to report you to the police."

I pocketed the pound coin and parked her car. Then I got in my car, gave Atkins a friendly wave and drove off.

On the way home I realised a further truth. That there are few lengths a person won't go to in order to save a couple of quid. Especially when it can go towards the cost of another pair of shoes.

****

June 15 2017. *COMPUTER VIRUS.*

It never ceases to amaze me why a person contacted on the telephone by a complete stranger allows them access to their computers. But apparently it happens all the time. I don't know anyone who has admitted to falling for this sort of thing, but I know four people, mates at *The Grim Jogger*, who have been prey to these nuisance calls. Fortunately none of them were taken in and have managed to keep secret their bank details or whatever else the intruder was after. Three of them, as soon as they became suspicious, simply put down the phone. Teddy Bannister, a no-nonsense Sunday league football referee, blew his whistle down the phone, and with any luck called full time on the caller's eardrum. Personally I would have welcomed such a call, it would be a golden opportunity for a bit of phone fun, the phone being my second most popular choice when it comes to the question of deriving fun from an electronic apparatus. (The first being when, as teenager, I acquired from America a Wankee-Doodle-Dandy via the classified ads section of an imported *Captain Marvel* comic. But that's another story.) However, as I say, I have never had such a telephone call. Until, that is, early this evening. It went like this:-

PHONE RINGS.

ME: Hello?

CALLER: Mr Ravenscroft?

ME: Yes?

CALLER: Your computer is infected. But don't be alarmed, stay calm, we can sort it. Go to your computer and turn it on.

ME: I don't have a computer.

CALLER: What? According to our information you.....

ME: My wife has one.

CALLER: Good. Please, get her to turn it on as a matter of urgency.

ME: Well I'll tell her but she won't like it, she's about to set off for the chippy.

CALLER: Stop her! This can't wait. Her computer is infected with a virus. Unless immediate action is taken important personal information such as her bank details and her password will fall into the hands of others who will use them to their advantage. They may already be doing this.

ME: I'm sure it can wait until she gets back from the chippy.

CALLER: No! It can't. Is she there?

ME: She's just putting her coat on, the one I got her for her birthday. It's a sort of greeny grey, with a black fur....

CALLER: Tell her to stop and turn on her computer!

ME: (CALLS) Love? Man on the phone wants you to turn on your computer. (ON PHONE) She says she's going to the chippy.

CALLER: Stop her! Stress to her it is vitally important she turns on her computer without delay.

ME: (CALLS) He says you have to do it now, Love. (ON PHONE) She's moaning about it, but she's doing it.

CALLER: Good. Tell her to press key F9.

ME: (CALLS) He says to press key F9. (ON PHONE) She says 'Are you sure this can't wait until she gets back from the chippy?'"

CALLER: Has she pressed F9 yet?

ME: (CALLS) Have you pressed F9? (ON PHONE)

She's pressed F9.

CALLER: Ask her what she's getting.

ME: (CALLS) He wants to know what you're getting. (ON PHONE) She says fish, chips and mushy peas for her, steak pudding, chips and mushy peas for me, salt and vinegar on both. But I could have told you that.

CALLER: (SILENCE, THEN PATIENTLY) *Ask her what she's getting on her computer screen.*

ME: (CALLS) He wants to know what you're getting on your computer screen. (ON PHONE) She says nothing.

CALLER: She must be. She should be getting instructions telling her what do next.

ME: She knows what to do next.

CALLER: What?

ME: Call in at the corner shop and get two of their oven bottom barm cakes to eat with our fish, chips and mushy peas and steak pudding, chips and mushy peas. We always have them, they're lovely thickly spread with Lurpak, not the normal Lurpak, that spready Lurpak, normal Lurpak is too hard, if you try to butter your oven bottom barm cake with normal Lurpak it disintegrates, you rip it to bits, I've complained to Lurpak about it but I don't suppose they'll do anything. Well they're Danish of course, so what do you expect.

CALLER: (AFTER LONG SILENCE) Are you *sure* she pressed F9?

ME: F9? I thought you said F5?

CALLER: No! *F9*.

ME: Are you sure?

CALLER: YES!

ME: There's no need to shout, if you start shouting at me I'm going to put the phone down.

CALLER: No! Sorry. Ask her to press F9. Please.

ME: (CALLS) Love? It isn't 5, it's 9. (ON PHONE) She says she wishes you'd make your fucking mind up.

CALLER: Has she pressed it?

ME: Yes. I'll ask her what she's getting, shall I? If she says 'fish, chips and mushy peas for her, steak pudding, chips and mushy peas for me, salt and vinegar on both' I'll ignore it and ask her what she's getting on the screen, shall I?

CALLER: Please. Please do that.

ME: (CALLS) What are you getting on the screen, Love? (ON PHONE) She says nothing.

CALLER: She must be.

ME: She says she isn't.

CALLER: Ask her if she's absolutely sure she pressed F9.

ME: (CALLS) Are you absolutely sure you pressed F9? (ON PHONE) She says she definitely pressed F9. First she pressed the F, then she pressed the 9.

CALLER: *No!*

ME: What?

CALLER: *She has to press the F9 key, not the F and 9 keys!*

ME: (CALLS) You've to press the F key, not the F then the 9. (ON PHONE)

She says she hasn't got an F9 key.

CALLER: *Of course she's got a bloody F9 key!*

ME: You're swearing! I'll put the phone down if you swear at me again; I don't like people swearing at me. I'm not having it, I'm old.

CALLER. Sorry! Sorry!

ME: Nobody swears at me. Nobody. Nobody at all. Well the wife does. If I've eaten all my steak pudding and ask her for a bit of her fish. She doesn't like that. Do you ever do that with your wife, eat all yours then ask for a bit of hers?

I kept it going for another five minutes then just put the phone down, leaving the line open. It could have been worse for him I suppose, I could have blown a football referee's whistle in his earhole.

****

June 17 2017. *MRS PALLISTER REVISITED.*

"I need your help," said Atkins. "Desperately. It's her again, Mrs Pallister."

This surprised me. "The lady still has designs on you? I'd have thought the sight of Carol-Ann in your arms would have got through to her that a romance with you is pretty much impossible."

"It's *her* fault," said Atkins with a scowl. "*Your* Carol-Ann. She blew the whistle on me."

The story came out. On seeing Carol-Ann leaving my house Mrs Pallister had buttonholed her, told her she ought to be ashamed of herself, that she was young enough to be Atkins's daughter, and had made it clear in no uncertain terms that she should be seeing men of her own age and leaving the pursuit of much older men to much older women, such as herself. Carol-Ann had replied that it would be her pleasure to do this as she had since discovered that Atkins was nothing less than a dirty old man. Apparently the news that Atkins was nothing less than a dirty old man had inspired Mrs Pallister into trying to get for herself a piece of whatever dirty old men get up to, and had been trying ever since.

"You've got to help me, Razza," Atkins pleaded. "I just can't keep her away."

"She still comes to your door armed with lasagne for two, I assume?"

"Oh no. No she's gone up market from that. It was beef bourguignon and a bottle of Cote de Nuits last night."

"Was it a good year?"

"What?"

"The Cote de Nuits?"

It doesn't take much to make Atkins's hackles rise and they rose now. "Look, I'm in deep shit here. And all you can do is go on about whether a bottle of wine is a good year?"

I looked at Atkins with suspicious eyes. "I hope it hasn't entered your head to enlist the services of my daughter again, and you're using me as a pimping service?"

"What? No, of course not. Who do you think I am?"

"I know who you are, Atkins, that's why I'm asking."

"Well I'm not. Besides, she wouldn't do it again, or she wouldn't have said what she did." A moment passed then Atkins said, too pointedly for my liking. "I was thinking perhaps...?"

"Perhaps what?"

"If she were to take a shine to someone else?"

"I hope you don't mean me?"

"Just to divert her away from me for a bit, like; just to give me bit of breathing space."

"Out of the question. Besides, she would never go for me."

"Why not?"

"Didn't you notice on your way in? There's a sign in the front window 'Leper Colony'."

Atkins almost believed me. "There isn't!"

"No, but there will be if you send her round here toting her lasagne."

Having failed to coerce me Atkins went back to pleading with me again. I told him I'd see what I could come up with but I wasn't promising anything.

In bed that night I considered the possible options open to Atkins. One would be to move house, preferably to an altogether different town miles away. However that might be expensive, and looking at it selfishly I wouldn't want Atkins to move as despite his occasionally getting out of control I enjoy his company. And who else would I get to play daft games with me? I toyed with the idea of Atkins making himself more unattractive to Mrs Pallister. However I soon dismissed it as a non-starter since I couldn't understand what Mrs Pallister found remotely attractive about him in the first place - taking it to its logical conclusion Atkins making himself even more unattractive could end up with him being even more attractive to her than he was in the first place. I thought about perhaps doing a repeat of what Atkins had done with Carol-Ann. But that would mean getting an attractive, much younger woman than Mrs Pallister to take my daughter's place. With the best will in the world I couldn't see Atkins attracting one. Perhaps a prostitute could fill the bill? It could, but in doing so it might present other problems, one being where would Atkins get one from? I'm sure he would have no idea, as nor would I. Then again, if he did manage to acquire the services of a lady of the night it would present other problems. Knowing Atkins as I do he wouldn't be satisfied with just succeeding in his mission to put an end to Mrs Pallister's interest in him; having paid for a prostitute he would want full value for his money, require his fill of her services, possibly bringing in its wake the contracting of some nasty sexually transmitted disease or other, accompanied by all the baggage this brings with it. I know for a fact that he would be loath take precautions as he once told me that on the only occasion he had used a condom it was like washing your feet with your socks on.

A couple of days later the answer came to me. Atkins would have to bite the bullet and invite Mrs Pallister into his bed. However, having got her there, he would discover that he wasn't able to perform, he would be unable to get an erection. A man without an erection is like a ship without a sail, and if he was unable to set out and sail before docking successfully in the widow Pallister's harbour then she would have no further interest in him. Job done.

Atkins was beside himself with joy when I told him. "Of course! Why didn't I think of that!" were his words. In view of what happened next I wish that he had.

I didn't hear from him for two or three days, which surprised me as he had intimated that he was going to get down, if not dirty, with Mrs Pallister that very night. So I rang him.

"How did it go?"

"*How did it go*?" The timbre of his voice told me things had not gone to plan. "*How did it go? I'll tell you how it bloody went.*" He paused, and cursed. "That bloody Christina!"

"What?"

"Christina! I've *only* gone and shagged her, that's all."

"Shagged Christina?"

"What? No, Mrs bloody Pallister!"

"You did it with Mrs Pallister?"

"Yes! How many times do you want telling!"

"Just calm down will you, get a grip on yourself and tell me what happened."

There was nothing but silence down the phone for seconds. Probably Atkins was debating with himself whether to impart the details or not, but eventually he said, "Well we went upstairs. I was hoping to do it, I mean hoping to be unable to do it, with the light out and as many clothes still on as possible, but no sooner is she in my bedroom than she starts stripping off. "*Let's do this thing right, Richard*, *honey*," she says, and strips off bollock-naked in no time."

"A strip but no tease."

"Shut it. Mrs Pallister naked is not a pretty sight. She is even wrinklier than I thought she'd be. Tits like two empty envelopes. The only good thing about it was that I wouldn't have been able to get a stiffy even if I'd wanted to. Anyway she lies on the bed and pats the duvet. I suppose you could say she patted it invitingly but I didn't feel in the least invited. But what could I do? So I get on the bed beside her. I reach for the bedside lamp to switch it off. She says, "*Leave it on, I like to see what I'm getting.*" This, I think, is a woman who has been round the block more than once. I steel myself and get on top of her. She wraps her arms and legs around me, she squeezes. There is no reaction from below. Nothing. But she's looking at me and I don't like her looking at me so I shut my eyes. Probably because she thinks I've shut them in passion she starts to squirm about underneath me. Then....I mean she is a woman after all, and it's a long time since I've had a woman underneath me, that feeling of your bare flesh on their bare flesh, your body interlocking with theirs....anyway, I'd watched *Bargain Hunt* as usual at lunchtime and Christina was on, lovelier than ever, and for some reason when I shut my eyes I started thinking about her and....well in no time I'd got a hard on up to my chin, and...."

I let this sink in before saying, "How was it?"

"*How was it? Never mind how it bloody was, she was round again the following night for more, and again last night, that's all you need to know! So help me!*"

Well I'll try of course, but it sounds to me that Atkins's situation may now be well beyond help.

Even my help.

****

June 20 2017. *CHEF.*

"Hi there, Plumber."

"Hi, Plumber. How's tricks?"

"What's that you're doing, Plumber?"

"This, Plumber? I'm fitting a new ballcock to this water cistern, Plumber."

"I can't help noticing that you're using a wrench, Plumber."

"Yeh. Rusty joint wouldn't you know, Plumber. Spanner refuses to shift it, Plumber."

Could anyone imagine, even in their wildest dreams, the above conversation ever taking place? People addressing each other not by name but by their profession? I don't think so. Yet chefs do it all the time.

"Hi there, Chef."

"Hi, Chef. How's tricks."

"Fine. What's that you're cooking, Chef?"

"This, Chef? Lamb's liver marinated in eastern spices, with a twist, Chef."

"I am assuming the liver is from a free range lamb, Chef?"

"Would I use anything else, Chef?"

Why do they do it? Salesmen and Engineers and

Solicitors manage to converse with each other without addressing each other as Salesman, Engineer or Solicitor all the time. (Although I believe some solicitors have started addressing each other as Arsehole, which is quite understandable.) So why then? To make sure we are aware they're chefs? We know they're chefs, we can *see* they're chefs, they're wearing the chef's white tunic, the black and white check trousers and the big white hat, why else would these prima donnas of the pots and pans be dressed like that? To fly an aeroplane? To deliver the post? At least if they insist on addressing each other as Chef they could make it a bit more interesting. Something like:-

"Hi there, Chef. Hmm, that smells delicious. It's your starter, Chef?"

"It is indeed, Chef. However, before my starter, I shall be offering an *amuse-bouche*."

"An *amuse-bouche*? What's that, Chef?"

"You're a chef, Chef, and you don't know what an *amuse-bouche* is, Chef?"

"Is....is it a vagina, Chef?"

"A vagina? What makes you think an *amuse-bouche* is a vagina, Chef?"

"Well I've been amused by quite a few vaginas, quite a few bushes, in my time, Chef."

"I didn't say bush, Chef, I said *bouche*. It's French. Literally an *amuse bouche* means 'mouth pleaser', Chef."

"I've been amused by a few mouths too, Chef."

****

June 22 2017. *MRS PALLISTER REVISITED AGAIN.*

The other day Atkins called round, still troubled by the attentions of Mrs Pallister. "You're going to have to help me get her off my back, Razza, things are getting desperate."

My friend looked quite put out about it. But I'd already tried to help him twice, so despite my feeling sorry for him I had no trouble in pointing this out.

"It'll be third time lucky," he said in reply, "I've always believed in third time lucky."

"I wish I shared your confidence. I wouldn't be confident even if I had another idea, after what transpired following my last two potential remedies to your problem. But I haven't." I paused for a moment to alter the mood. "Perhaps we've reached the time when you should just give in to the woman gracefully, accept the situation with dignity? Are you still having intercourse?"

High horses don't come any higher than the ones Atkins spoke his next words from. *"STILL having? What do you mean STILL having?"*

"You aren't then."

"I never was *still* having intercourse with her! There's no *still* about it, I had it with her *once*."

"Sorry, there's no need to bite my head off. I was only asking."

"Well don't." The anger in his voice was replaced in equal measure by sarcasm. "I mean that's really going to put her off me isn't it, shagging her? That's *really* going to put off a woman who is hinting every five minutes that she wants our 'relationship', as she calls it, to continue."

"She's still very keen then?"

"Keen isn't the word. Gagging is the word. Last night she rang the bell in her nightie."

"She has a bell in her nightie? What's that for, to signal to you when to start and stop?"

"Will you bloody stop it!" The anger was back. The sarcasm hung around to accompany it. "You can never forget you used to write jokes for a living, can you. Crap jokes too if they're anything like that one."

"Sorry, force of habit. What did she say? When she came round in her nightie?"

"She said, would you believe, *"I'd just got ready for bed when I realised I'd run out of bread. Well I didn't want to go to the trouble of getting dressed again just to pop round for a slice of bread, and I really can't do without a piece of toast with my breakfast."* Can't do without a piece of my dick now and then, more like it."

I shrugged in sympathy. "Well I'm sorry for you, mate, really I am; but we've already tried everything I've been able to come up with."

"There must be *something*?" Atkins's winsome expression put me in mind of a faithful spaniel appealing for its dinner.

"Well if there is I don't know what it is."

I thought about it for a moment or two. "Perhaps if there was something about your house that made it uninviting to her?" I clutched at a straw. "Maybe she's allergic to cats? If she's allergic to cats you could get a cat."

Atkins shook his head. "No, that's no good, I don't like the bloody things either, so....*mice!*"

"What?"

"Women don't like mice! I'll tell her I've got mice, that'll get rid of her! They hate mice, women, the sight of a mouse scares them shitless. Meg once jumped up on the table when she saw one."

Atkins could have hit on something. The Trouble had been the same; she'd run a mile if she saw a mouse. I said, "I think you've got it Atkins my boy; tell Mrs Pallister your house is overrun with mice and she'll never darken your doorstep again. In her nightie carrying a lasagne or otherwise."

Atkins frowned, seeing a snag. "But she's been in my house, hasn't she. A few times. Too many times. She's been in my hall, my living room, my kitchen, my bedroom; she knows I haven't got mice."

I shrugged this off easily. "So we'll get some."

"Where from?"

"Would you believe a pet shop? A pet shop is bound to have mice. About a dozen should do the trick."

Atkins remained doubtful. "They'll be white though. She won't believe it if they're white; white mice won't take her in, she'll think they're pets."

"She'll still be scared of them though, they're still mice."

"Possibly. But not necessarily. Kids keep white mice as pets; she could have had one as a kid. Learned to love it. I had one myself. I used to keep it in a shoebox until I got fed up with it and put it down the waste disposal unit."

"You put your pet mouse down the waste disposal unit?"

"I wanted to see how quickly it disposed of it." He caught my shocked look. "Well I was only about seven, kids do things like that at that age, I had an inquiring mind."

"I'm beginning to understand why you chose to become an income tax inspector for a living."

"We could dye them I suppose?"

"What?"

"Yes, we could dye them," Atkins repeated, warming to his idea. "It shouldn't be a problem; I dyed Meg's hair for her the time she fell and broke her arm getting the coal in. There was nothing to it."

"Yes but she wasn't running around in a shoebox when you were trying to dye her, was she, as the mice will no doubt be doing."

Atkins's confidence remained unshaken. "I'm sure we'll manage. I can hold them down while you work in the dye. We'll pick some up at Boots on the way to the pet shop."

There were lots of colours to choose from at Boots and we spent a bit of time deciding which colour was the most mouse-like. The assistant, a frosty-faced woman, or at least she would have been if she hadn't been wearing about a month's supply of cosmetics on her face, was no help at all when we asked her advice. All she offered us was a funny look - anyone would have thought it was odd that someone would want advice on mouse-dyeing. We couldn't decide between

Garnier's Nutrisse Intense Dark Brown and their Nude Dark Brown. In the end we decided on a packet of each. Atkins wanted to add a Nude Dark Blonde, giving us four mice of each colour 'for a bit of variety' but I told him this was gilding the lily a bit.

In the end it was a waste of time and money because when we got to the pet shop we found that not only did they have white mice but had mouse-coloured mice as well. We bought a dozen, and after a futile attempt by Atkins to get his money back at Boots we returned home. Atkins took no time in inviting Mrs Pallister round and told her to bring her nightie.

This morning he rang me up. He didn't have to tell me how it had gone, his voice told me. It had gone wonderfully. Mrs Pallister, on seeing the mice, had fled, never to return.

"Where did you put them?" I asked. "In the kitchen?" I had advised Atkins that the kitchen would be best, being the room where mice mostly put in an appearance, via the skirting boards.

"No."

"Where then? In the living room?"

"No."

"In the bedroom?"

"In the bed."

"In the bed?"

"Well I didn't want them to get trampled on; she could have trampled on them in her rush to get out if I'd let them loose in the bedroom," said Atkins, revealing a compassion for mice he must have developed since he put his pet mouse down the waste disposal unit. "You should have seen

120

her face when I flung back the duvet and there were twelve mice sat there. You should have heard the scream."

"I can imagine."

"Frightening. One of the mice shat itself; well it must have, there was no shit there when I tucked them in for the night."

"Too much information, Atkins. Where are they now, the mice?"

"I gathered them up and turned them loose in the garden, gave them their freedom. Far better than being cooped up in a pet shop waiting for someone to buy them and keep them in a shoebox."

Atkins had put the mice in the bed for fear of them being trampled on. Now, in another act of compassion he had turned them loose to live life as nature had intended. Was my friend turning in a saint?

****

June 24 2017. *THE HAKA.*

Twenty-three huge men dressed in black shirts, black shorts and black socks are lined up in three rows. At a signal from one of them they stick out their long tongues in a rude manner, drop into a semi-squatting position, their arms pointing in opposite directions across their chests. It looks very much as though they are about to begin a display of formation tea-bagging. But they all look angry, fearsome, eyes stuck out like chapel hat pegs. Why are they looking so angry? Maybe it's because they've been tipped off that the people they are about to tea-bag are going to bite their bollocks halfway through the tea-bagging? No, it isn't that. In fact the men aren't formation tea-bagging at all, they are the All Blacks, the New Zealand Rugby Union team, and they are about to perform the Haka, an ancient posture dance performed by the Maori, the indigenous people of New Zealand. Apparently the Haka is a challenge to the opposing side to meet them in battle. Today the opposition is the British Lions. The Haka begins, the All Blacks chant, in loud, threatening, demented voices:-

Ka Mate! Ka Mate! Ka ora! Ka ora!
Ka Mate! Ka Mate! Ka ora! Ka ora!
Tenei te tangata puhuru huru
Nana nei I tiki mai
Whakawhiti te ra
A upa...ne! ka up...ne!
A upane kaupane whiti te ra!
Hi!

What do these strange words mean? I haven't a clue. At a guess I would say, *"All right then, it's us lot against you lot, but it's our ball, so if you start beating us we're going home and taking it with us, and if you try to stop us we'll tell our dad, and our dad's bigger than your dad and our dad will kick your dad's arse, so stick that in your pipe and smoke it!"*

Perhaps not. I Google it. The words mean:-
I die! I die! I live! I live!

I die! I die! I live! I live!
This is the hairy man
Who fetched the sun
And caused it to shine again
One upward step! Another upward step!
An upward step, another... the sun shines!

Nothing in there about kicking your dad's arse and sticking that in your pipe and smoking it, then. Nor, more realistically in view of the way the New Zealanders often go about the game of rugby union in order to gain an unfair advantage, no mention of the dark arts of illegal tackling, blocking, spear tackling and holding a player back by covertly grabbing his shirt. Accompanying the words the All Blacks make with the body language. This consists of leaping up and down, thumping the floor with their fists as though beating the opposition to a pulp, and shaking their clenched fists in various manners. One of the clenched fist gestures looks very much like the one British men do when they see a woman and indicate to a friend that they would very much like to have sex with her. Another one seems to be calling the British Lions wankers.

The Lions watch the performance stone-faced, silent. If I were their captain we would be doing a Haka of our own, a British Haka. Immediately the All Blacks started their Haka we would turn our backs on them, drop our shorts, stoop down and moon at them. Halfway through we would stick a hand between our legs and give them the V-sign. In its way this would be as traditional of Britain as the Haka is traditional of New Zealand, but without all the hairy man who fetched the sun bullshit.

****

June 28 2017. *ATKINS 2 TWO - THE RETURN OF THE BEST IDEA YET.*

Atkins has approached the independent British film company Baby Cow Productions with his 'best idea yet'. They told him to bugger off.

****

July 1 2017. *CELEBRITIES.*

"Give over, who do you think you're kidding? You'll never get eighty quid for that in a million years!"
"Oh no it bloody isn't!" Zap!
"Jesus wept, is there any programme those two pillocks aren't on?"
"Oh for Christ's sake get on with it, you two aren't half as funny as you think you are."

The above are just a few examples of me shouting abuse at the telly. The first is my response to a contestant, possibly blind, on *Bargain Hunt*, who bought a pot pig you wouldn't give a fiver for. My second is to a continuity announcer's news, or perhaps warning, that *"It is now time for Britain's Got Talent."* The third is my reaction to any appearance of Mel & Sue or Ant & Dec on my TV screen. The fourth is my spoken thoughts on the interminable inane 'banter' between Alexander Armstrong and his long friend on *Pointless*. I have yet to shout anything at *The Eurovision Song Contest* as after seeing it once, and a second time by accident when I was channel-hopping, I never switch on the telly when it's on in case I accidentally see it again.

I wish there was such a thing as a shite filter, an app you could attach to your TV that would filter out all the shite programmes. The problem with this though, for me, is that there wouldn't be very much left to watch as it would consign to its built-in rubbish bin all programmes with the word 'celebrity', or the name of a celebrity, in the title - a proviso that would automatically cut out about half the programmes on offer nowadays. Indeed a new programme need only have a limited success to spawn almost immediately a celebrity version. So we have *Celebrity Masterchef*, *Celebrity The Chase*, *Celebrity Big Brother*, *Celebrity This, That and the Other*, and, most appropriately, *Pointless Celebrities*. Has ever the coming together of two words been more apposite? It can only be a matter of time before we'll be able to tune in to *Celebrity Weather Forecast*. And I'm convinced that if anyone came up with the idea of a programme all about celebrities, called *Celebrity*, that it would be turned down because they wouldn't be able to follow it up with a celebrity version.

In addition to the above we have a host of programmes fronted by celebrities. There are hundreds of them; *Chris Tarrant Goes Fishing, Robson Green's Wild Swimming Adventure, Paul Merton's Secret Stations, Griff Rhys Jones's*

Greatest Cities of the World, Joanna Lumley's Japan, Caroline Quentin's National Parks, Caroline Quentin's Supermarkets, Caroline Quentin's Back Garden, Caroline Quentin's Navel Fluff, et al. (All right I've made up the last three, but there is time.) I have no wish to see *Ant & Dec Swim with Dolphins.* I wouldn't mind watching *Ant & Dec Swimming with Sharks and being Eaten by them.* You can put me down for that. I would give my right arm to see it - as long as the sharks took both arms, legs, heads and torsos of Ant & Dec. In fact I have no wish to see Ant & Dec, nor Mel & Sue, nor any other celebrities, doing anything on television other than the things they have become famous for, and certainly not programmes fed to the viewers on the conceit that just because Martin Clunes or Griff Rhys Jones or Adrian Edmondson or someone else who should know better is doing something, that it will be more interesting than if someone you've never heard of is doing it. In an ideal world there would be no *Robson Green goes Clog Dancing, Chris Tarrant goes Brass Rubbing* or *Joanna Lumley goes Robson Green and Chris Tarrant Rubbing,* to besmirch the nation's TV screens.

Despite all these celebrities, apparently there aren't enough of them to go round. More must be found to guest on *Celebrity This, That and the Other.* There is already evidence of the bottom of the barrel being scraped. Recently my TV guide named the five celebrities in *Celebrity Mastermind* who were to take to the famous black leather chair. I hadn't heard of a single one of them. The black leather chair was more famous. I was once asked by someone I have known for ages if, in view of the fact that I once wrote for TV and radio and had written a few books, if I considered myself to be a celebrity. I nearly hit him. Although, thinking about it now, and in view of the celebrities listed in *Celebrity Mastermind,* maybe I am.

All the people I have named above are 'Celebrities'. The dictionary definition of the word celebrity is 'A famous person, especially in the world of entertainment or sport'. Well that may have been the case at one time. Today you can become a celebrity just by being on a TV programme; you don't have to be good at anything. I once saw a fourteen-year-old star-struck schoolgirl break off from sucking her thumb to say in a vox pop interview that her ambition was to be a celebrity. It was not to set out on the path to becoming a singer, a ballet dancer, a musician, a tennis player, a footballer, and by hard work and good fortune become good at it, *become* a celebrity; she just wanted to be a celebrity. She has every chance of success. Nowadays celebrity bars no one. Jade Goody, a contestant on *Big Brother*, became a celebrity for being thick. It wasn't long before producers of reality shows, never slow to see mileage in something, had a thick person in their show; Joey Essex in *The Only Way is Essex,* Chloe Ferry in *Geordie Shore,* every 'reality' show had one. Thick was good. Incidentally, why 'reality' show'? They should be called 'unreal' shows; it's certainly a reality I've never come across.

I do like a good rant. If I can convince myself that I'm a celebrity I may do a celebrity version later.

****

July 4 2017. *10 THINGS ATKINS WANTS TO DO BEFORE HE DIES.*

"Have a look at this, tell me what you think," said Atkins, handing me a piece of notepaper.

"What is it?" I was wary; I don't like Atkins handing me mysterious pieces of notepaper, it seldom ends up to my advantage.

"My bucket list. Ten things I want to do before I die."

"Is murder Mrs Pallister on it?"

"Don't tempt me."

I glanced at the list. "Swim with dolphins?"

"Yes, I've always wanted to swim with dolphins."

Whether dolphins would want to swim with Atkins is another matter but I didn't mention this, contenting myself with asking him why he wanted to swim with dolphins, in preference to, say, sardines.

"Well it must have something going for it," he replied, "it's on everybody's list."

"I've never seen the appeal myself."

"Apparently dolphins are very intelligent."

"There you are then, you have nothing in common."

"What? Oh yes, very funny I'm sure."

I looked at the next item on the list. "Do a parachute jump?"

"Yes I've always fancied doing a parachute jump."

Atkins and I are cut from the same cloth, which is why we have become such good friends. However when it comes to things like broadening one's experiences I tend to err on the side of caution whereas Atkins errs on the side of foolhardiness, if not downright stupidity at times. I looked at him sternly. "Atkins, you are seventy-nine years old, you're the same age as me; I know we're both still in reasonable nick but there is a limit."

He brushed this aside. "There's no age restriction, I've checked. The only proviso is that you have to be no less than four feet in height."

"You could very well be less than four feet in height about a second after you've landed."

"No, it's quite safe. I've been into it thoroughly. You come down with an experienced parachutist."

"What, you mean holding hands?" I raised an eyebrow. "It's not homosexual parachuting is it?"

"What? No, don't talk daft, you're strapped to him."

"Strapped to his back you mean?"

"To his front actually. You know, harnessed, like one of those harnesses women hang their babies from. It'll be like that but without the tits."

I shook my head gravely. "Rather you than me, Richard." I looked at the next item on the list. "Join the 5 Miles High Club?"

"Yes, I've *definitely* always wanted to do that. I could never persuade Meg." He reflected for a moment. "There was the time I was still single when I'd just about got my end in with a stewardess above the Pyrenees but we had to stop due to turbulence. But I don't suppose that counts."

"I wouldn't have thought so."

"But it must be a wonderful experience," he enthused, "sex at 30,000 feet. Well that's why it's on my list." He looked skywards as though visualising it, before going on. "Of course I shall have to organise somebody to do it with."

"You see not long back you could have enlisted Mrs Pallister, I'm sure she would have only been too happy to oblige. I mean you've already had sex with her at three feet. But unfortunately you've blotted your copybook there."

"True, but I'm bound to find somebody, I'm sure."

I had a thought. "Perhaps you won't have to?"

"No?"

"I mean if the bloke strapped to your back on the parachute takes a shine to you halfway down you could be joining the 5 Miles High Club whether you want to or not. And, incidentally, at the same time killing two birds with one stone. Strictly speaking it probably won't be five miles high but I don't think you need to let details get in the way."

Atkins looked genuinely worried. Like me he has never been able to fathom out the attraction some men have for other men's bottoms. Suffice to say that sex between two males isn't something we will be trying out for ourselves at some point. Leaving Atkins to his worries I moved on to the next thing on the list.

"You want to walk the Great Wall of China?"

"Yes."

"Assuming your bottom is all right after your parachute job, of course. I mean the last thing you want is to be walking it with a sore bottom."

"In view of what you said I shall be taking precautions on the jump. Three pairs of underpants should suffice."

"I don't think you've thought this Wall business through," I said doubtfully.

"What do you mean?"

"Well it takes you all your time to walk to the Chinese chip shop down the road, never mind the Great Wall of China. Have you any idea how long it is?"

"No. Long."

"Very long. It's said it is the only man-made object you can see from space; so it's safe to say it's a lot longer than the trip from your house to the Chinese chippy."

"We're only going to be walking the touristy bit."

"What?"

"We're only going to walk the touristy bit."

"We?"

"I was thinking we could do it together. Along with the other things on your ten things I want to do before I die list. Assuming that walking the Great Wall of China is on it of course."

"It isn't. And I don't want to do anything before I die."

"What?" said Atkins in disbelief. "Everybody wants to do something before they die."

"I don't. Everything I've ever wanted to do I've already done."

"There must be *something*?"

"No."

Atkins knew better. "I thought you wanted to get the legover with Kristin Scott Thomas?"

"I do, but that's hardly likely to happen, is it?"

"You never know."

"I'm not changing my bed sheets daily in readiness."

"But you'll come with me when I do mine, will you? We can make a holiday of it; you can watch me while I'm doing them, you can be a spectator."

I remained non-commital and glanced again at the list. "You want to learn to ride a horse?"

"Yes."

"Well that should be worth seeing. After your attempts at equestrianism on that donkey at Blackpool. I'd have thought that would have put you off riding anything with more than two legs for evermore."

"Well I'd had a drop too much to drink, hadn't I; I shall be learning to ride a horse cold stone sober. And I really need to be able to ride a horse; it could very well help me to achieve another thing on my list, appear in a film. Especially if it's a cowboy picture. I might have to settle for being an extra, I can't expect a Brad Pitt role, I realise that, but that's still being in a film. It's on my list, isn't it? After having a tattoo?"

"You intend to have a tattoo?"

"Yes."

"Where?"

"Stockport. There's a place on Underbank."

"Where on your *body*?"

"Oh. On my arm probably; just the one arm, that seems to be the fashion. I was thinking the Niagara Falls. It will look rather spectacular cascading down my arm. Maybe with a man in a barrel going over the top of it."

"The arms on which tattoo artists usually perform their skills are young arms, arms that are smooth," I pointed out. "Yours are all wrinkled."

"The wrinkles will make it look like the water is shimmering." One thing I will say for Atkins; he has never lacked for imagination.

In addition to the things I've already mentioned he intends to ride the Big One at Blackpool, visit Old Trafford to watch Man U play in a big game, pose nude for a life class and take the train journey on Scotland's West Highland Line from Fort William to Mallaig. I totted them up. "There's twelve things here."

"I might back out of the tattoo and the nude modelling. So what do you say?"

"Possibly I'll go to Blackpool with you when you go on the Big One. I might even go on it myself."

"There you are!" said Atkins, delighted. "I told you there was something you wanted to do before you die."

"I don't want to do it before I die. But if you're doing it, and I feel in the mood, I might. I might also accompany you on your railway trip on the West Highland Line. And a Man U game is a definite."

Atkins beamed. "Great. When do you want to start?"

I was already beginning to have misgivings. I'd forgotten Atkins and Blackpool, a place where he seems to lose entirely what few inhibitions he has, as he had ably demonstrated when he rode a donkey into the sea brandishing a toy wooden sword he'd pinched from a kid and shouting *"Hurrah for England and St George!"* at the top of his voice, which ended in a fight with the donkey's owner.

We shall have to see.

****

July 6 2017. *WIMBLEDON.*

The Wimbledon Tennis is upon us once again, bringing with it, as sure as winter follows autumn, blanket coverage of the event on BBC Radio Five. For me, this is even worse than the blanket coverage they gave the General Election, when I had to resort to tuning in to TalkSport to avoid listening to some dim politician or other going on about how wonderful it was all going to be when his or her party was elected. At Wimbledon time, if I switch on Radio Five, my ears are assaulted by either the thwack of tennis balls being hit - accompanied to squeals of delight from the crowd if they happen to have been hit by a British player who has about as much chance of winning the championship as I have of becoming the next Pope - or the very latest news on Andy Murray's hip or whatever else is plaguing the happy Scotsman at the moment. But I can't even listen to TalkSport now because half the time it's on that as well.

Naturally the event is getting the same amount of coverage, if not more, on the BBC TV channels. Being kind, I don't suppose you can blame the BBC for their love affair with tennis as apart from synchronised swimming and dominoes it's just about the only sport they have left since Sky and BT purloined all the football, cricket and golf. But tennis all day, every day?

Oddly enough I used to like Wimbledon. I couldn't get enough of it; sat there in front of the telly with my strawberries and cream and a glass of Pimms I was quite in my element. Oh all right then, a cup of tea and an Eccles cake. I can identify precisely the time I began to stop liking it and what stopped me from liking it; June 4 1971, on the first appearance at the All England Club of the American Jimmy Connors. And the thing that stopped me liking it was Jimmy's grunt. I had never heard the like before. Nor had anyone else in this country. Up until then tennis players had just hit the ball and left it at that. Occasionally, and understandably if it was a long game, you might get a grunt of exertion during a long rally. With Jimmy you got a grunt all the time. At first he confined the grunt to his serve, with just the occasional grunt during a rally. Very soon, maybe because he kept winning his matches and thought that the addition of a grunt was a contributing factor, he grunted with every stroke of his racquet. At that point he made a subtle change, a change that was to reward him with even greater success: instead of grunting just after he hit the ball he started grunting just before he hit it. This seemed to confuse Jimmy's opponents - possibly on hearing him grunt it upset their timing and they tried to hit the ball before it had the chance to arrive - but whatever it was it resulted in Jimmy winning his matches more easily. Jimmy then started mixing up his grunts, some before his stroke, some after, and some both, a ploy that made him even more successful. (There was a rumour going round at the time, and I see no reason to doubt the veracity of it, that an opponent complained to the Wimbledon authorities that Jimmy's array of grunts put him into such a state of confusion that on at least four occasions he had tried to hit the grunt instead of the ball.)

At this point the Wimbledon authorities should have taken Jimmy to one side and had a quiet word with him, but for reasons best known to themselves they chose not to, and thus ruined tennis for me and thousands of others. Because soon after that other tennis players, taking note of Jimmy's success, built a grunt into their own game. In next to no time most tennis players were grunting. I used to think Jimmy's grunt was bad but that was before I heard Maria Sharapova's grunt. Compared to Maria's grunt Jimmy's grunt was a whisper in a lover's ear. In fact Maria's grunt isn't a grunt at all; it's more a blood-curdling shriek, the sort of sound I imagine a pig makes when it dawns on it that it is just about to have its throat cut.

These days many tennis players grunt and shriek. If you were to walk past the All England Club at anytime during Wimbledon fortnight, and the crowd noises were removed, no one would argue with you if you were to say that it was like walking past a pig abattoir at slaughtering time. Perhaps the BBC, instead of covering Wimbledon, could instead do an outside broadcast from just such an abattoir and save itself a lot of money?

At a push I could tolerate aberrations like Henman Hill, Murray Mound and probably, if she manages to get beyond the third round, Johanna Konta's Mound of Venus, but I'm afraid that, for me, grunting will always be a toleration too far. Konta, incidentally, the 'British' hope, is about as British as Kim Jong-un. Cynic that I am I can't help wondering if, when she applied for British nationality, if instead of being a very promising tennis player who might one day win the Wimbledon Women's Championships she had been a one-legged Bangladeshi who didn't know one end of a tennis racquet from the other, we would have rolled out the welcome mat so readily. In fact it wouldn't surprise me if one day an Amazonian gorilla with a half decent serve and volley game turned up at Wimbledon HQ and was fast tracked for British nationality.

Oh, and another reason I don't watch Wimbledon nowadays, equally important, is that the ladies have replaced their panties with what appear to be cycling shorts. The spoilsports. If they'd gone the other way and started wearing G-strings I might well have been able to put up with all the grunting and squealing.

****

July 11 2017. *CYCLISTS.*

Today I had a letter published in the *Sunday Times*. In last week's edition their chief sportswriter David Walsh wrote a pioneering piece aimed at encouraging drivers to show more tolerance to cyclists. My letter, prompted by this doubtful plea, read as follows:-

Reference David Walsh's rant on the rights of cyclists. Perhaps motorists would show cyclists more respect if, in slow-moving traffic, they abided by the rules of overtaking, and therefore didn't habitually put the shits up motorists by overtaking them on the inside.

In fact the man in charge of reader's letters edited out the words 'put the shits up' and replaced them with 'scares'. This from a newspaper that regularly prints f*** and c*** for you know what. However, even after this chicken-hearted and totally unnecessary use of the red pencil, I think I made my point.

I might have some sympathy for David Walsh's views if the vast majority of cyclists were of the opinion that traffic lights applied to them as well as cars and lorries, and were happy to leave the pavements to pedestrians, for whom they were intended, but they aren't.

I wrote my letter from sad experience. Like all motorists I have been plagued for years by cyclists overtaking me on the inside in slow moving or stationary traffic, or 'undertaking' as it has come to be known. (Possibly because those doing it are inviting the services of an undertaker.) On one occasion, after a cyclist had done this to me four times, the next time the traffic ground to a halt I got as near to the kerb as I could, no more than six inches, in an effort to stop him doing it a fifth time. The ignorant bugger only banged on my roof and remonstrated with me! Naturally I ignored him. Before winding down the window and giving him an earful.

I have often thought, on seeing the approach of a cyclist about to overtake me on the inside, how I would dearly love to lean over and push open the passenger door, causing him to run slap bang into it. Sadly, even at my most mean, I knew I would never be able to bring myself do this. Then one day, out of the blue, it was done for me. I was in stationary traffic yet again when I saw an acquaintance, Bob Greening, standing at a bus stop. I wound down the window, called to him and asked where he was going. He said home, and as it was on my way I told him to hop in. The traffic was alternating between slow moving and stopped. A cyclist overtook me on the inside. On the move again the traffic ground to another stop after a mile or so. Bob said, "We're only a hundred yards off, I'll nip out here." Unknown to Bob the cyclist who had previously overtaken me on the inside was in the act of doing it again, and no sooner had Bob swung open the door than there was a squeal of brakes and the cyclist went gloriously arse over tip, over the handlebars, over my car door, and fell in a heap about five yards up the road. He staggered groggily to his feet, shaking his head to clear it, clutching a shoulder in pain, blood dripping from one of his knees. It was quite wonderful. Bob got out of the car, I bade him goodbye and drove on.

When I got home I inspected my car door. There was a bit of damage to a hinge, which was to cost me eighty pounds to put right. I would happily have paid double.

****

July 19 2017. *BBC PAY*.

Today the BBC revealed details of salaries in excess of £150,000 paid to the presenters, stars, and celebrities on its payroll. No sooner had some of these people, especially the women, found out they were being paid less than half the salary paid to some of the others for doing much the same job, came the sound of more noses being put out of joint than if the entire field of the *Tour de France* had fallen off their bikes and landed on the tarmac face first. Gary (Mr Mogadon) Lineker, a man who sits on the fence with more regularity than a hundred years old crow with its arse nailed to the top of one, worth £1,800,000 a year? I wondered how the powers that be arrived at such a preposterous amount.

SCENE: The BBC Salaries Board is meeting to discuss their stars' salaries. Present are Lord Smog, Mr George Quango, Sir Hugh Sinecure and Mr John Sensible.

QUANGO: Next on our list is....er....Gary Lineker, gentlemen.

LORD SMOG: Which one is he?

SENSIBLE: He presents Match of the Day.

LORD SMOG: Just Match of the Day? Nothing else?

QUANGO: Well we did once try him at the golf. The Open I believe. Apparently he made a proper dog's breakfast of it. Viewers switched off in droves, so we haven't risked trying him with anything else. Oh and I believe he once co-hosted that Sports Personality thingy we do every year, the time we couldn't get the one who stutters.

SINECURE: How much are we paying Lineker at the moment?

SENSIBLE: One million eight hundred thousand per annum.

LORD SMOG: Seems a lot just for presenting Match of the Day?

QUANGO: He does do it every Saturday. Only in the football season of course; he has the summer off.

SINECURE: Even so. How much are we paying that Balding woman?

LORD SMOG: We have a bald woman presenting our programmes? Oh I don't like the idea of that, not at all; it's bad enough having the ones with hair.

QUANGO: No, Balding, Lord Smog. Clare Balding.

LORD SMOG: Never heard of the woman. What does she present?

SENSIBLE: Oh, show jumping, three day eventing, all the Olympics sports, the Wimbledon tennis, athletics, yachting, the Boat Race, just about everything.

LORD SMOG: And she puts the kettle on and makes the tea for the camera crew as well, I assume?

QUANGO: Oh I'm sure her hundred and fifty thousand a year will include making the tea, Lord Smog. It will be in her contract, no doubt about that.

SENSIBLE: Even so, it isn't even ten per cent of what we're paying Lineker. I think we need to put his salary in perspective. A consultant surgeon is paid a hundred thousand pounds per annum. Which is eighteen times less than we're paying Lineker. I don't know about the rest of you but if I had to undergo heart surgery I would far rather a heart surgeon do the operation than Gary Lineker.

QUANGO: That's hardly fair, Sensible. I mean Lineker isn't a heart surgeon is he.

SENSIBLE: No, and I would be the first to agree that a heart surgeon wouldn't be able to present Match of the Day as well as Gary Lineker does. But whereas it would take forever and a day to train Lineker in heart surgery a heart surgeon would be able to fulfil Lineker's role perfectly satisfactorily given a couple of weeks or so on the job. As would most people and not a few chimpanzees. In fact they'd probably do it better; by all accounts he isn't very good at it.

SINECURE: This Lineker chappie? Isn't he the one who advertises potato crisps? I mean I've got shares in Walkers and they do very well, we don't want to go upsetting the man.

QUANGO: And he _is_ a role model for the young of course.

SENSIBLE: Right. Having seen him advertising crisps they stuff their faces with them and end up walking around like tubs of lard.

QUANGO: Perhaps we should put this one on the back burner? The next one on our list is Chris Evans. Whoever he is.

LORD SMOG: He isn't another of those shit stabbers we have taken to employing nowadays, is he?

QUANGO: Thankfully I believe he's one of the few who still bat on our side, Lord Smog.

****

July 22 2017. *THE WORLD'S GREATEST INVENTIONS.*

THE WHEEL

THE NAIL

THE PRINTING PRESS

THE LIGHT BULB

THE CONTRACEPTIVE

THE INTERNET

THE PLOUGH

THE TELEPHONE

THE STEAM ENGINE

THE COMPUTER

According to an internet website the above is a list of the world's greatest inventions. I beg to differ. For one thing it doesn't list *the* greatest invention. I could put up a decent argument against some of the other inventions being named in preference to it too. For example The Light Bulb. Now I would be the first to admit that a light bulb is very useful; if it wasn't for light bulbs everyone would spend a large part of their lives groping about blindly in the dark, and not just the British Government. However a light bulb's disadvantages are not to be glossed over. For example if I ever have to go to Wales again the last thing I want is for it to be artificially lit during the hours of darkness; the less I see of Wales the better following the experience of my only two other visits to the Principality, documented at some length and with great regret in my other *Stairlift* books.

I could also put up a strong case for excluding The Nail from the list. Which is not to say that the humble nail is without value. Indeed, when a leg has departed company from the MFI table you bought last week a nail is exactly the thing you need to replace whatever they used to secure the leg in the first place in the forlorn hope that it would stay attached to the rest of the table for more than five minutes. Then again, if it wasn't for the nail most of the joiners employed on building affordable housing would have to go to the trouble of learning how to use a screwdriver. But there is a hefty price to pay for having the benefit of nails to secure things. Specifically, take the case of Jesus. If it hadn't been for nails he could never have been nailed to the cross. *"Octavio, I need a little help here, ...Yes, he's fallen off again. I mean it's all right for sticking notes to the fridge door but Blu-Tack does have its limitations, this is a fully grown human being we have here........Yes I've tried fastening him up by his long hair but he says it hurts. I tell you*

144

what, get me some Araldite, we'll see if that'll keep him up there."

The Contraceptive. I couldn't put up much of an argument that contraceptives shouldn't be included in the list. I could find fault with the earliest forms of stopping unwanted babies, the most successful of which was a barrelful of crabs with a hole bored in it, on the grounds that although it did what it said on the tin it not only stopped babies but stopped just about everything else. However modern methods of contraception, be it condom, pill or diaphragm, are virtually foolproof ways of preventing unwanted offspring. And available to everyone, except of course for those of the Catholic faith who have managed to keep themselves honest, who must still leave the cinema before the end of the picture. But that's their lookout.

The Computer, although a positive boon, is by no means a perfect invention, as anyone who has had their internet banking account cleaned out will agree. Along with another of the inventions, The Internet, it gives access to anything you would want to know about everything (and, if you accidentally hit the wrong key, quite a few things you would rather not know). But in doing so it also tells maniacs all they need to know about making bombs with which to blow up innocent people. So by no means an entirely good thing.

The Telephone is another invention which has both good and bad points. It's good that you can speak to someone miles away at any time you wish, bad because you can't speak to someone miles away at any time you wish because all their lines are busy at the moment and you are in a queue and two weeks later you're still in the queue mouthing oaths and tearing your bloody hair out.

The Printing Press, The Wheel, The Steam Engine and The Plough I can happily go along with as I love to read, drive, travel on steam trains and do the odd bit of ploughing.

So what *is* the greatest invention in the world? The TV Remote of course. All day long. What a truly wonderful, wonderful invention it is. I can't praise it too highly. It has a channel swapping facility you can take advantage of whenever you've forgotten to switch over after watching the evening news on the BBC and your ears are suddenly assaulted by that shrieking woman presenter on *The One Show*. It has an on/off button, which you can immediately call into service whenever a party political broadcast or Alan Carr or the National Anthem comes brash and uninvited to your television screen. (I haven't heard more than the opening bars of the National Anthem for at least five years; just the time it takes to either switch off or switch over to something more uplifting such as a particularly bad weather forecast.) It has a fast forward facility to get rid of all the adverts, provided that, like me, you have recorded in advance all the ITV and Sky programmes you are interested in watching. (The last advert I watched featured the Milky Bar Kid.) It has the marvellous mute option, which allows you to enjoy watching the football without having to listen to yet another uneducated commentator say, along with whatever else banal rubbish he comes out with, *"Chelsea are all in blue"* when he means *"Chelsea are in all blue*". So it's possible that half of them are in blue and the other half in red is it, you silly man? It has a subtitle function which allows you to know what the actors in dramas are saying, which nine times out of ten you can't because they're mumbling, or even on the odd occasion they aren't mumbling their voices are drowned out by mostly unnecessary and always overloud music. But best of all you can use the mute and subtitle functions in tandem, which enables you to watch brainboxes like Professor Brian Cox and Lucy Worsely (the latter from behind the settee, admittedly, especially if she's got herself tarted up in some period costume or other) without having to listen to them.

The TV Remote - what could possibly be a better invention?

****

August 3 2017. *MAN BREASTS*.

"This, I have got to see," said Atkins. "I'm coming with you next time you go."

Atkins, like me, has seen man breasts before. (You have only to venture onto a British beach in the summertime to see almost as many man breasts as woman breasts. Spoiler Alert! *If you don't want to see man breasts avoid Skegness.*) Unlike me, however, Atkins had never seen man breasts that were as pert and shapely as the breasts of a well-developed young woman. The breasts in question, when I first saw them, were initially in a bra, were naked for a moment or two, thereafter in a bikini top.

I am learning to swim once again, partly because The Trouble had always wanted me to in case I ever fell into the canal (ever more likely the older I get), and partly because several people have told me that my reportage of the first time I tried to learn how to swim was the funniest bit in the first of these *Stairlift* books. It wasn't funny for me, as I recall, but in the hope of hitting on something else worth including in these pages I had enlisted for lessons again.

It was in the changing rooms of the swimming baths at the local leisure centre that I saw the wonderful man breasts that Atkins, as keen a breast man as you could hope to find, was so anxious to get an eyeful of. They were on a thirtyish man, not overweight - unusual with man breasts as they can mostly be found on fat men - but not in any other way attractive; a moustache, beard and breasts not being the most appealing combination of features. He had a pleasant enough face though, nice skin, and more hair, black and lustrous, than quite a few women. I first saw his breasts two weeks ago, prior to the first of the ten swimming lessons that would transform me into an English version of Johnny Weissmuller but without a knife between my teeth and the absence of crocodiles. I saw them again the following week, although the second time not in their naked state. The man had made no effort to cover them up, and if he hadn't taken off his bra and replaced it with a bikini top I would have said he was totally unaware of their existence.

"You can already swim," I pointed out to Atkins, when he said he was going to join me.

Atkins insisted. "I'll pretend I can't. I'll splash about, I'll make out I'm drowning, I'll call for somebody to chuck me a life belt, I'll do anything I have to. *I have to see those breasts!*"

I could see there was no stopping him, and after lying through his teeth and signing on for the course Atkins accompanied me to my next swimming lesson. When we arrived the changing room was empty.

"I hope we haven't missed him," said Atkins with a worried frown.

"He won't be behind the lockers," I said.

"I was just making sure."

"Besides, even if we've missed him you'll see him in his bikini."

"Oh no," said Atkins, shaking his head. "I want to see the lot. The full Monty. Bra, removal of bra, naked breasts, putting on of bikini top."

Just then Man Breasts walked in. I shifted my eyes in his direction and gave a furtive nod.

"Is that him?" said Atkins, in a stage whisper, all agog. I indicated it was.

Atkins and I were already in our swimming trunks, so in order not to be seen just hanging about whilst Man Breasts got changed we did a few arms stretch knees bend warming up exercises. As before, he disrobed to reveal he was wearing a bra. When he removed it Atkins was so transfixed by the sight of his wonderful breasts that he suddenly stopped warming up whilst in the knees bend position and fell over. After scrambling to his feet mumbling apologies, but not for one moment taking his eyes off the wonderful breasts, he continued to warm up (in more ways than one, I suspect). Man Breasts put on a black bikini bra, a match for his bikini bottoms, and made for the pool.

"Well?" I said to Atkins. "Was I right or was I right?"

"You were right. Dead right and then some."Atkins rolled his eyes. "What a pair of knockers, eh. Tit heaven."

"I've been thinking about it," I said. "It could be that he's transgender; maybe he's going through the process of becoming a woman?"

"Well I hope I'm around when he gets there," said Atkins. After a moment he said, "I might ask her if she'd like to join me in my 5 Miles High ambitions."

During the swimming lesson Atkins positioned himself so close to Man Breasts it was almost obscene, clearly in the hope his bikini top might come adrift and he would get another look at his bare breasts, but he was out of luck.

The following week Man Breasts failed to put in an appearance. I suggested to Atkins it was probably because he didn't fancy the prospect of being stalked again. When he didn't turn up again the week after, at Atkins's insistence I asked the swimming instructor if she knew why. Apparently he has moved to Leeds and will be continuing his swimming lessons there. No doubt to the delight of any men of Leeds who are currently learning how to swim. I don't think it will be long before Atkins asks me to go to Leeds with him.

****

August 10 2017. *MEMORIES OF AN EIGHTY-YEAR-OLD NEXT BIRTHDAY - GROWN UP.*

I am twenty-two. Eighteen months ago I returned home to England after completing National Service, most of it in Germany. While I was over there for the best part of two years the only German words I picked up to add to the only one I already knew, Hitler, are bier and zigaretten. My pronunciation of them is near perfect. Since my demob I have been working in a plastics factory. In the 1967 film *The Graduate* a man tells the Dustin Hoffman character that plastics is the future. It isn't mine. One of my workmates is called Derek. Derek is a bit backward. As a schoolboy he had what is known in today's politically correct times as 'learning difficulties'. (When I first heard this expression I wondered what it meant, in what way did a child have learning difficulties? Did the teacher blindfold him? Make him wear ear plugs? Make him do his lessons with his head in a bucket?)

Some of my workmates take the piss out of Derek. His tormentor-in-chief is Eric Berry. Derek goes *'to t'pictures'* every night, come hell or high water. Aware of this Berry asks him what's on at the Essoldo this week. Derek replies with the name of the film, say, *The Jolson Story*. Berry shakes his head and says, *"No, you're wrong there, Derek, the roof's on at the Essoldo."* Derek grins his silly, innocent grin and says, *"No, it's you what's wrong, Eric, t'Jolson Story is on at t' Essoldo. Seen it last night, it were dead good."* Berry insists. *"No, it's you who's wrong, Derek, the roof's on at the Essoldo."* To give Derek a clue as to what the joke is Berry then looks up at the roof and reiterates, *"The ROOF is on at the Essoldo."* And so it goes on for minutes on end. Derek never gets it. Another. Berry: *"What's on at the Plaza this week, Derek?"* Derek: *"t'Ten Commandments.* Berry: *"What's it about?"* Derek: *"Moses."* Berry: *"Who the fuck's Moses?"* Derek: *"Charlton Heston."* Berry regularly sidles up to Derek, strokes his behind and says in a conspirational voice, and to the amusement of all: *"What's your BOTTOM price, Derek?"* I must have seen him do it a hundred times. Today Derek thinks that he himself will be the instigator of the amusement. He sidles up to Berry, strokes his behind and says: *"What's your LOWEST price, Eric?"* Priceless. Everyone curls up. Me, I'm ashamed to say, included.

*

I am thirty. I am in a classroom with eleven other employees of Bowater, the paper manufacturers. We are on a two week Foreman & Supervisor course in Northfleet, Kent. Sitting next to me is Walt, a Yorkshireman, the only other northerner on the course. For this reason, and because we have been housed at the same hotel in Gravesend, we have become friends. The night before last, the eighth day of the course, we had a few pints together in a local pub. Afterwards, watered but not fed, we called at a fish and chip shop. Walt declared his fish and chips *"Just abaht passable if th'art non bothered what they taste like."* and complained bitterly that no mushy peas were available. On our way back to the hotel our conversation got round to our favourite foods. Walt's are all very plain; liver & onions, steak and kidney pie and mash, egg and chips, mutton pie and gravy, and, naturally, Yorkshire pudding. *"Wi t'roast beef, and for afters too, smothered i' syrup."* I was surprised then that when we decided to dine out for a change, rather than eat at the hotel where it was already paid for, Walt suggested a Chinese restaurant. He explained: *"I've never had a Chinky but our Jimmy had one once an' he's still above ground to tell t'tale."*

We took our seats in the restaurant, *The Perfumed Garden*. Walt remarked that he had never been in a garden that smelt anything like it, *"It smells more like t' pig bin at back o'Barnsley Co-op"*, but he was prepared to give it a go. I studied the menu. Walt ignored it. I thought perhaps, as he hadn't been to a Chinese restaurant before and would be unfamiliar with the dishes on offer, that he was leaving the ordering to me. A waiter arrived and asked if we were ready to order. I ordered sweet and sour pork with fried rice. I was about to ask Walt if he fancied the same but before I could the waiter beat me to it. Below is their conversation.

"Chicken"

"Chicken?"

"Chicken."

"What sort chicken? Sweet sour chicken, chicken with noodles, chicken with black bean sauce....?"

"Just chicken."

"Just chicken?"

"Just chicken. A whole one."

"Whole chicken?"

"A whole chicken."

"What sauce? Sweet sour sauce, hoisin sauce, black....?

"No sauce."

"No sauce?"

"Just a whole chicken. Plain."

And that's what Walt had. He ate the lot, skin and all, and sucked the bones dry. *"I like to get me full value, ah've paid good brass for it."* On the way out he told me that Chinese food wasn't as bad as he thought it was going to be and he might visit *The Perfumed Garden* again before he left.

Now, in the classroom, we are having a break between lectures. Robert, a fellow supervisor, is holding forth yet again. I disliked Robert from the moment I met him, as did Walt. Robert is far too large for me, not large as in big, but large in full of himself. Everything with Robert is 'the old'. *"Me and the old girl got the old bikes out over the weekend, called in at the old pub for a spot of the old lunch, had a plate of the old jellied eels, lovely."* Robert works at the nearby Bowater Scott factory where they manufacture toilet rolls, 'Scotties' paper handkerchiefs and paper sanitary towels. One day last week we had a conducted tour of the factory. Robert was in his element, proud as punch of his place of work. He regaled the rest of us at great and boring length about the products he was responsible for making. Now he is at it again. *"Did we realise Bowater Scott make over half the country's toilet rolls?"* Well if we didn't, we should, he's already told us three times. *"Did we realise 'Scotties' outsold all other brands of paper handkerchiefs by more than two to one?"* We did, for the same reason. *"Did we know that the old girl said Bowater Scott's sanitary towels were the best she had ever used?"* We did but would rather we didn't. *"Did we realise that Bowater Scott....?"*

Walt chose this moment to raise a hand, stopping Robert in full flow. Having stopped him he said, *"And does thee realise, Robert, that everything Bowater Scott makes yer can either blow yer nose on it, wipe yer arse on it or stick it between yer legs?"*

Robert was a bit more humble, certainly less large, after that.

*

I am thirty-five. With The Trouble I am in the Winter Gardens Opera House, Blackpool. (This is the occasion I have reason to be grateful to Blackpool for, mentioned previously.) We are there to see *The Ken Dodd Laughter Show*. I am not looking forward to it in particular; I have seen Doddy on TV and as a comic he's all right, no more. But it's something to do. How wrong I am. On stage the man is magic. Gag upon gag upon gag, rat-a-tat-tat, so quick fire that soon I am laughing so much, as is everyone else in the audience, that I scarcely know what I'm laughing at. After being onstage for two hours Doddy looks at his watch and says, *"Well, we're about half way through."* Doddy's performance teaches me a lesson too, in a roundabout way. Although I knew that I could never be a comic - I have always been able to amuse my friends but I could never in a million years stand on my own on a stage facing an audience of two thousand, charged with making them laugh, I'm not brave enough; I'm not being paid to make my friends laugh, it's different, an audience have paid good money, if they didn't laugh at my first joke you wouldn't see me for dust. But I have funny thoughts, observations on life, a way of saying things in a funny way, much like Ken Dodd has. It dawns on me that I could maybe become a writer of jokes, a comedy scriptwriter.

A couple of weeks later I send Doddy a page of one-liners that might suit him. He writes back - I have no telephone - telling me that he likes some of my stuff and would I care to come along and see him at his home in Knotty Ash, Liverpool. *Would I!* A week later I turn up at his house, or the house where his directions have led me too. But it can't be his house, Ken Dodd is a big star and big stars live in big posh houses not little red brick cottages filmed in coal dust with a coal yard round the back. Ken Dodd does. It turns out the coal yard belongs to his dad, Arthur, at well over seventy still bagging and flogging sacks of coal to the neighbourhood despite his son's fame and fortune. I knock on the front door. Doddy himself answers it, not the maid I am still half expecting, despite the coal yard. Welcoming me warmly he ushers me into his front room, seats me in a chair, tells me he'll be with me in a minute, he has to deal with something first. I don't see him for another two hours. I will soon learn that he has about as much respect for time as he has for income tax returns. Doddy's front room is by far the untidiest room I have ever seen. Apart from an area of about three feet by two feet leading into the room the entire floor space is full. There are floor to ceiling stacks of yellowing old TV and radio scripts, the majority of them with added cobwebs, stacks of books old and new, most of them dusty. There is a brass band big drum and several other musical instruments including an alpenhorn. Another drum, a tympani, has a black cat sat on it, licking itself and looking at me suspiciously every now and then. There are about two dozen tea chests brim full of everything; pots and pans, a mangle like my mother used to use, a number of multi-coloured watering cans, a baby's carrycot. Three of the tea chests are full of tickling sticks. What must be a coffin, judging by the brass handles, is filled to overflowing, grotesquely, with smiling Diddy Men dolls. Sitting there amongst it I wonder what I have let myself in for. I have let myself in for a cheque for £20 for the gags I have written thus far (almost half of my current weekly wages at Ferodo Brake Linings at the time), with the promise of more to come if I shape up. *I am a writer!*

*

I am thirty-six. It is eleven in the evening. The Trouble and me will soon be off to bed, The Trouble already has her nightie on. There is a knock on the front door. The Trouble looks at me; who on earth can that be at this time of night? She slips on her dressing gown and together we go to the door. I can't open it as earlier in the week I nailed it up, it has a dodgy lock and won't close properly, it needs a new one and I haven't had chance to get one yet. Another knock on the door, more urgent. I lift the letter box flap and speak. "Who is it?"

A voice outside says "It's Doddy."

I turn to The Trouble. "It's Ken Dodd."

She is nonplussed, as am I. "I wonder what he wants?" she whispers.

"Probably his money back," I reply, not completely joking.

"Well let him in then," says The Trouble with a mixture of impatience and foreboding. I remind her that I can't open the door and say I'll tell him to go round the back. She is beside herself. "You can't tell Ken Dodd to go round the back, he's Ken Dodd!"

"Well I can't just leave him there, can I."

"You'll have to go round and get him, it's pitch black out there, we can't have him walking into our dustbin, he's Ken Dodd."

I go round to the front door with a torch and lead Doddy back. On the way he tells me he has been doing a function in Congleton and is on his way back to Liverpool.

The previous week I had written to him to say I wouldn't be sending him any more gags. Working up to sixty hours a week in a factory to do my best by The Trouble and our three young children left little spare time for writing gags, and it had all got a bit too much for me; I'd already been in trouble with the foreman for 'daydreaming'. Now, settled on our settee with a coffee, he urges me to carry on, do what I can when I can, I have talent, I shouldn't throw it away. He quotes one of the lines I'd written for a routine he was doing about the great variety stars of days gone by: *"My father was an old time great - my mother used to blacklead him."* That, he says, is talent, it's surreal and daft, an ideal combination, it's *funny*. I promise Doddy I'll carry on sending him gags. He goes on his way, leaving three Diddy Men toys for the kids.

Over the next few months, before throwing in the towel again for other reasons, I find time to both write and to accompany Doddy to a few TV and radio shows and personal appearances. Two in particular stand out. The first was at the BBC Manchester TV studios where he was guesting on a magazine programme fronted by Stuart Hall, before it came out that he was Stuart-keep-your-fourteen-year-old-daughter-out-of-sight-Hall. I took an immediate dislike to him, all the backslapping and false bonhomie, so I must be a good judge. The other time was when Doddy was providing the after-dinner entertainment at the annual dinner of a cricket club in Leek. It was after ten-o-clock before his services were called upon and by then the audience of about two hundred cricketers and their friends were well oiled and getting more than a bit rowdy. I wondered how he would cope with them. Doddy got to his feet, looked around, and said with a hopeful look*: "They told me this is where I can get my stumps drawn."* He had them immediately. A great, great comic.

*

I am forty. I am at the BBC Television Centre in the office of Peter Whitmore, the producer of *The Two Ronnies*, soon to be the producer of *The Dawson Watch*, Les Dawson's second series for the BBC following his move from Yorkshire Television. (The first series, a shared show with

Lulu, had not gone down too well and had been axed.) For the past couple of years I have been sending gags and sketches to various comedians, shows, with limited success. One of my successes was sending in 'news items' for *The Two Ronnies*, the funny cod items of news with which they topped and tailed their show. I was encouraged by the Ronnies' script editor Ian Davidson to try writing a sketch for them. I wrote two, they liked and used one of them. Because of this I was invited by Peter to send in material for Les's new show. I did.

Now, Peter tells me he is going to commission me for ten minutes material for each of six *The Dawson Watch* shows. This is equal to six months wages at the Bowater Drum factory, where I am currently employed (for the second time). *I am up and running. I am off!* The following day, taking a chance on getting more commissions in the future, I pack in my job and become a full-time comedy scriptwriter. There is a saying that life begins at forty. It did, career wise at least, for me.

*

I am forty-three. I have been a full-time comedy scriptwriter for just over three years and today I am busy, busy busy: I am the script editor and co-writer, along with Les Dawson, for *The Les Dawson Show*, whilst at the same time script editor and writer on *The Marti Caine Show*. It's more work than I would want but I soon found out that in the scriptwriting business it's often either feast or famine - you have to take the work when it's there because just around the corner there may be no work at all for a week or two.

This morning I am at the BBC rehearsal rooms in North Acton, rehearsing Les's show.

Although by now I have had several sketches on *The Two Ronnies* I had never met the Ronnies. When I discovered they were rehearsing in the next room I put this right. As luck would have it when I walked in on them unannounced they were rehearsing one of my sketches, 'Big Blue Book'. Feeling a bit self-conscious about it I introduced myself. Ronnie Barker and Ronnie Corbett were charm itself, generously telling me how funny my sketch was and how well they knew it would go come showtime. I was really made up - most scriptwriters, whether commissioned or otherwise, try to get scripts on the Ronnies show; when I got my first one accepted a couple of series ago I really knew I had what it takes.

One of the guests on Les's show this week is the heavyweight boxer Frank Bruno. Up close Frank is huge, a gentle giant. When I shook hands with him my hand literally disappeared. Number nine shovels are smaller than Frank's hands.

We rehearse the sketch he is doing with Les. It's a simple affair as sketches go, with little dialogue, a boxing match between Frank and Les (billed as 'The Great White Hope') for Frank's British heavyweight title. Before the bout commences Les boasts that despite his having had more than one hundred fights he has managed to keep all his teeth. *"I'll prove it if you don't believe me."* He produces a matchbox, rattles it, opens it: *"Here see, I keep 'em in here."* Fellow scriptwriter Andy Hamilton, with whom I worked on *The Dawson Watch* (Andy's first TV job too) and *The News Huddlines*, once said to me that you can't go wrong with a sketch that makes fun of the star. Les's boxing match verified this truth.

The fight consists almost solely of Frank stood in the centre of the ring, his huge gloved hand flat on Les's head, holding him at bay as Les attempts to hit him. As Les is no more than five feet four inches tall whilst Frank is at least a foot taller this is never going to happen, even when, frustrated with his attempts, Les stomps out of the ring only to return wearing a pair of gloves the size of two leather pouffes. Still unable to hit Frank, Les finally throws in the towel, literally, by going to his corner, taking the towel from round the neck of his second, and tossing it into the ring. His second recovers it and tries to shove Les back. A fight breaks out between Les and his second. Les can't hit the second either. Reluctantly he goes back to fighting Frank. The fight ends with Les being disqualified when, attempting a roundhouse swing at Frank's jaw, he turns through a hundred and eighty degrees and lands the punch on the referee, knocking him clean out of the ring.

Next we rehearse a sketch set in a police station in which Roberts, a midget, played by Big Mick, applies for a job as a policeman. Les, in a characterisation of Robb Wilton, plays the desk sergeant.

LES: How tall are you, Mr Roberts?
ROBERTS: Six foot. A shade under six foot.
LES: How tall?

ROBERTS: Two foot ten.

LES: You see, Mr Roberts, being brutally honest about it, you're not really tall enough to be a policeman, are you.

ROBERTS: Please. Please, Sergeant. I've set my heart on a career in the police force. One day I hope to be known as Roberts of the Yard.

LES: I think that's highly unlikely. I mean you're not even a yard of Roberts.

Les's other guest on the show is the American singer Bertice Reading. Bertice is big, black, and jolly, a real Red Hot Momma of a lady. Often one of the duties of a script editor is to write some light-hearted chat for the part of the show where the star welcomes on the guest. If the dialogue isn't going to sound stilted and unnatural this is a far from easy task. Some scriptwriters must find it beyond them, otherwise you wouldn't get exchanges like: *"Say, that's a nice polo neck sweater you're wearing there, Tom. Tell me, do you by any chance play polo?" "Well I did until one day I nearly drowned, Englebert." "You nearly drowned? Playing polo?" "This is water polo I'm talking about here."* I swear this is true.

Having said that, writing natural sounding dialogue for Les and his guests is comparatively easy, as whatever I come up with Les's ad-libs soon kick in to make the whole thing sound spontaneous even though it isn't. I am able to add an ad-lib of my own occasionally. In rehearsals yesterday I added a gem.

Bertice and Les had met for the first time and were getting on like a house on fire. It soon became clear that no input would be required from me - Les would welcome Bertice on to the show and they would just get on with whatever came into their heads as far as they and I were concerned. Whilst they were joshing with each other Bertice insulted Les, calling him *"A sawn-off John Bull, with the accent on the bull."* Countering this insult Les retorted, in his grand, affronted W.C. Fields manner, *"How dare you come onto my show and abuse me! Just who do you think you are, you American hussy!"* In an inspired moment I added to Les's words: *"Stood there like the Three Degrees."* Bertice curled up. *"Yuh'll do for me, Terry mah boy, yuh'll do for me."* and slapped me on the back, nearly flattening me in the process. (For those who may not know, The Three Degrees were at the time a very popular black girl singing group, still going today I believe.)

Today Bertice fails to appear for the final rehearsal. She eventually arrives when, having rehearsed everything else and having waited for her for over an hour, we have given up the ghost and are about to leave. She apologises profusely. Then gives the reason for her lateness. I will never forget her words, possibly the best excuse, certainly the most unexpected, I have ever heard. *"Well ah was about to set out but all of a sudden ah gets the itch."* She winks and digs Les in the ribs. *"Y'know what I mean. And when ah's got to be fucked ah's got to be fucked, so ah gets mah man to give me a good seein' to. And it's so good ah had him do it all over agin, and the tahme just flew."*

Bertice's late arrival leaves me running late

for my second script-editing duty of the day, drinks with Marti Caine and the guest on her next show, film star Diana Dors, at the hotel where Marti is staying. Diana, no singer but able to carry a song, is to do a duet with Marti. Following it they will sit and chat. I make it just in time and arm myself with a pen and notebook to record anything they say that we might use for their chat. Diana, at the age of fifty-one is still quite glamorous and extremely attractive, Marti equally so. I feel like a weed in a garden of roses. The two of them get on famously. I am, apparently, completely oblivious to them as they chat away like old friends rather than two people who have just met. They talk mostly about their childhood and their paths into show business. (Diana by appearing in a succession of risqué sex film-comedies before being signed at the age of sixteen by J Arthur Rank - who she said everyone referred to as J Arthur Wank - Marti by appearing on the Yorkshire club circuit as a stand-up comic and cabaret singer before rising to national prominence after winning the talent show *New Faces* in 1975.) Some of their chat is quite raunchy. Diana reveals that the people at J Arthur Rank asked her to change her surname. She supposed it was because they were afraid that if her real name Diana Fluck was up in lights and one of the lights blew they would be in trouble with the law. Marti reveals that one of the many impresarios, managers, agents et cetera who tried to feel her up on the way to inviting her onto their casting couch was none other than Hughie Green. No surprises there then. I am quite fascinated by it all, two beautiful, famous women sharing their mucky secrets.

After about a half hour of this has passed Marti sits back from the tête-à-tête and says she supposes it's about time they should start thinking about what they're going to talk about on the show. I tell her she must be joking. She asks me what I mean. I say, "You've just been doing it; do what you've just been talking about, people will love it. We might have to edit out the worst of the filthy bits before transmission but the studio audience will love it."

"Do you think we dare?" says Marti, wide-eyed.

"Of course we dare," says Diana. "If they don't like it, bollocks to 'em."

And that is what they did. The audience gave them a standing ovation. Much, much better than Marti complimenting Diana on her polo neck sweater and asking her if by any chance she played polo.

*

I am forty-six. I am sitting in the audience at the Paris Theatre, London, the venue where BBC Radio record many of their shows, comedy shows in particular. I am watching the recording of the pilot of my own show *Star Terk Two*, so named because, for contractual reasons, I wasn't allowed to call it *Star Trek Two*. (I have turned this to my advantage in the opening show when I have the crew land on the planet Dyslexic and Captain Kirk becomes Captain Krik and Mr Spock becomes Mr Pocks.) A sketch show, *Star Terk's* premise is that at the outset of each episode Captain Kirk and the crew of the Starship

Enterprise are somewhere in space on their five year mission to explore strange new worlds

MR SULU: Captain, Captain, the rear right-hand side of the Enterprise is covered in condoms!
KIRK: You don't mean....?
MR SULU: Yes - there's Klingons on the starboard bow!

About six minutes into their mission they are interrupted by a radio show. The rest of the thirty minutes is a series of linked sketches, the sketches themselves interrupted at one point by 'The Seventeenth Minute of the Show' which, surprise surprise, always happens seventeen minutes into the show. Tonight we have already passed the pilot show's seventeenth minute spot - the President of the National Union of Mineworkers Arthur Scargill reading the fairy story *Goldilocks and the Three Bears*. Performed by the wonderful Fred Harris, with a spot on impersonation of Arthur Scargill, it went down very well with the audience. Here it is in its entirety:-

Once upon a time there were Three National Union of Honeyworkers Bears. Father Socially Deprived Bear, Mother Socially Deprived Bear, and Baby Socially Deprived Bear. And they all lived together in a criminally highly-rented, rate-capped, damp, rat-infested, totally inadequate council house in the woods! One day, they all went off to picket at their local honey pit, as after eighteen years of Tory misrule they were grossly *underpaid and didn't have any alternative but to withdraw their labour <u>and take strike action!</u> Soon afterwards a girl by the name of Goldilocks, who was on her way to see her grandma, noticed the house of the three bears and went in. She didn't know it was wrong to go into somebody else's house without their permission as her father was a policeman and <u>she'd seen him do it many a time!</u> On the table were three bowls of porridge. Now in the past the three bears had been able to afford a substantial meal of meat stew and dumplings, but under the yoke of Conservatism, and I want to make myself very clear on this point, <u>porridge was all they could damn well afford!</u> First Goldilocks tried the porridge of Father Socially Deprived Bear, but that was too hot. Then she tried the porridge of Mother Socially Deprived Bear, but that was too cold. Then she tried the porridge of Baby Socially Deprived Bear, and that was just right. So she ate it all up. Then, not content with that, and with a black-hearted underhanded deviousness that would have done credit to Thatcher herself, she mixed together the bowls of too hot and too cold porridge and ATE THEM AS WELL! Then the wolf came in, and Goldilocks said "Oh Grandma, what a big mouth you've got." And the Wolf said "I know, I borrowed it from Neil Kinnock. And they all rotted in a hell of Conservative making.*

Seated by my side, metaphorically holding my hand, is the previously mentioned Andy Hamilton. I have much to be thankful to Andy for. In 1978, after we had finished writing the first series of *The Dawson Watch*, and although I was sending in scripts on spec to the various sketch shows that were accepting material at that time, I had no commissioned work to turn to. Andy, who had already written for radio shows *The News Huddlines* and *Week Ending*, introduced me to Griff Rhys Jones who was about to produce a new radio series, *Marks in his Diary*, starring Alfred Marks. On Andy's recommendation Griff commissioned me to write five minutes material for each of the shows. I was in work again. Eventually this led to me being asked to write for the long-running *News Huddlines*; a long and happy association with that programme and its star Roy Hudd ensued.

Huddlines, amongst other things, taught me how to write to a deadline. A topical show, whatever you wrote had to be about something that had been in the newspapers during the current week. The show was recorded on Wednesday lunchtime for transmission the same evening, meaning that you had two days at the most to come up with something. This was in the days before email, even before fax, so the only way I could submit my minimum of five minutes material was to travel down to London on the train from Manchester every Tuesday. I would stay overnight, put the finishing touches to my contributions in the *Huddlines* writers room the following morning, contribute a few of the one-liners for Roy's opening monologue, maybe write another sketch with Andy, then watch the recording of the show (again at the Paris) before returning home later the same day.

I remember one such trip to London in particular. I had already written one sketch the previous day. One of my better ones, it was based on a news item about a gravedigger who was also drawing the dole. It started:-

FOSTER: And just what do you think you're up to, Mr Nesbitt?

NESBITT: What? Oh, it's you - Mr Foster from the dole office.

FOSTER: I asked you what you think you're doing?

NESBITT: Me? Why, I'm gardening Mr Foster.

FOSTER: In the graveyard?

NESBITT: Yes. You see what with me being on the dole the vicar lets me have this little corner to grow my own veg and flowers.

FOSTER: These here are your flowers are they?

NESBITT: The tulips, yes. They've got a lovely bloom on, haven't they.

FOSTER: They've also got a card of deepest sympathy from Bert and Gladys on.

NESBITT: That's right. They bought them from me. I was going to tell you so you could knock it off my dole, the first chance I....

FOSTER: Never mind that. What's that hole for?

NESBITT: That? It's for my early King Edwards.

FOSTER: Six feet is a bit deep for potatoes, isn't it?

And so on.

On the train down I completed writing another sketch about the World Snooker Championship being contested at the time. It was prompted by news of an incident involving the grossly overweight Canadian player Bill Werbeniuk, a player noted for the copious amounts of lager he consumed before and during matches - at least six pints before a match and then one pint for each frame. (No fool he, Bill successfully claimed the cost of ten pints of lager per match as a tax deductible expense.) During one of his current matches, in stretching over the table to play a shot, Bill had split his trousers at the back from waist to groin. My sketch was about the other players in the championship drinking large amounts of alcohol whilst playing and coming to grief in various manners. Soon I had the sketch but didn't have Roy's funny little preamble to set it up. I had spent more time thinking about it than I did writing the sketch but still hadn't come up with anything worthwhile. *"And what about that snooker player Bill Werbeniuk splitting his trousers, eh? They say he did it leaning over the table to play a shot but personally I think he was stretching to get his hands on another pint of his tax free lager."* Not funny enough. *"....apparently they could hear the sound it made as far away as the Lake District."* Not funny at all. So on and so on. And then, out of the blue, it came to me. I wrote:-

ROY: And what about snooker player Bill Werbeniuk splitting his trousers, eh? Apparently he didn't know until he realised there were three pinks on the table.

Now, the pilot of *Star Terk Two* is almost over. It has pleased the audience, I'm relieved to say.

There have been quite a few belly laughs, 'knee slappers' as fellow *Huddlines* writer Laurie Rowley calls them. One of the knee slappers was in the closing sketch, set in a travel agency. (A man sat two places along from me actually slapped his knee!) The travel agent had met each of a customer's choices of holiday venue with a sharp intake of breath and a good reason why anyone with any sense wouldn't even think of going to such a country for a holiday:-

CUSTOMER: You wouldn't recommend Spain either then?

TRAVEL AGENT: Mosquitoes, sir. Mossies as big as aeroplanes. You'd get bitten to death.

CUSTOMER: Yes I'd heard mosquitoes could be a bit of a problem in Spain now you come to mention it. I'll plump for Italy then.

TRAVEL AGENT: (SHARP INTAKE OF BREATH)

CUSTOMER: What's wrong with Italy?

TRAVEL AGENT: Nothing if you don't mind spending your entire holiday sat on the lavatory. I'll never forget the holiday I had in Naples. 'See Naples and die'? See Naples and diarrhoea more like.

CUSTOMER: Hmm. How about Bulgaria then?

TRAVEL AGENT: (AN EVEN SHARPER INTAKE OF BREATH)

CUSTOMER: No?

TRAVEL AGENT: Just the opposite of Italy. Constipation. When I went there I was bunged up for the entire two weeks.

CUSTOMER: Yes, well I can certainly do without

that. I suppose I could try Greece?
TRAVEL AGENT: Well I tried everything. Syrups of figs, senna pods, cascara, a tyre lever....
CUSTOMER: No, for a holiday! Greece the country. I mean.

The show comes to an end. The cast take a bow. Then, quite unexpectedly, one of the actors, Jeffrey Holland, introduces me to the audience. I have to stand up to take their applause. I have never felt so self-conscious in my life. When I sit down the man sitting on my other side asks me for my autograph. Now I am embarrassed in addition to feeling self-conscious. But also quite pleased; I've never been asked for my autograph before. I sign with a flourish as though I do it every day.

Incidentally the entire two series of Star Terk Two can be listened to online, here:- fourble.co.uk/podcast/starterk

****

August 22 2017. *TALK TALK.*

I've had another call from Talk Talk's Man in the Orient. He's been calling me about once a month ever since Talk Talk took over the supply of my broadband connection about three years ago. I don't know what he wants because I always put the phone down the moment I realise who it is; I have never had an overwhelming desire to pass the time of day talking to someone from Talk Talk, definitely definitely. Under normal circumstances I usually restrict the plaguing of people who ring me uninvited in an effort to extract money from me by one dubious method or another to about once a year, as I don't wish to become bored with it. And it isn't all that long since I skewered the man who tried to get into my computer. But when Talk Talk's man rang this afternoon I wasn't feeling too well disposed to foreigners as South Africa were doing too well against England in the cricket for my liking, so I let rip on him. Our conversation went:-

"Yes?"

"Am I speaking to Mr Ravvenscrorft?"

I took a moment to reign in my natural inclination to tell him that if he couldn't be bothered to learn how to pronounce my surname correctly I couldn't be bothered to talk to him, then said patiently but firmly. "Mr *Ravenscroft*."

"Ravenscroft? My apologies, Mr Ravenscroft. I sometimes have a problem with the pronunciation of British names."

"No need to apologise, I've had a problem pronouncing Calcutta and Madras ever since they were changed for no good reason to Kolkata and Chennai. And you are?"

"I? I am Mr Singh."

"Then I will call you Mr Song. And you can continue to call me Mr Ravvenscrorft."

"That will not be necessary; I am OK with Ravenscroft, Mr Ravenscroft."

"As you will, Mr Singh, Singh."

"I am calling you from Talk Talk, your internet provider."

"I had guessed as much. How may I help you?"

"It is I who may help you, Mr Ravenscroft." This said with great pride.

"Oh yes?"

"Oh yes. For I am calling you about our special offers."

I thought about this for a moment. Could I perhaps pretend to have mistaken 'special offers' for 'special orifice'? Well of course I could. "Well there's a surprise, Mr Singh," I said in mock amazement. "And there was I thinking you were calling me about the bargain of a few more channels on my digibox for another fiver a week. Tell me, what shape does the special orifice come in? Round I suppose. And what purpose does it serve? Is it, perhaps, an extra anus, in case the other one wears out? An inconvenience that probably happens with some frequency in your part of the world, Mr Singh, what with all that spicy food. But you said it was a *special* orifice. What's special about it? Could it, perhaps, be an earhole that suddenly becomes deaf whenever Coldplay come unexpectedly onto my radio and returns to working normally when their noise is over and done with? Or maybe it's a nostril that can sniff out a financial adviser bearing a dodgy pension plan at a hundred paces ? If so, you can put me down for either and with the minimum of delay. Or, even better, is it an arsehole that can fart music, such as the famed anus of Le Pétomane, the Frenchman who could fart the French national anthem *La Marseillaise*? In which case, and with due regard to my dislike of the Monarchy, I would be able to fart *God Save the Queen* whilst still retaining a degree of disdain. I want more details of your special orifice, and at once, Mr Singh, for I am in a state of excitement at the prospect of it."

A long moment passed. "I do not understand what you are talking about, Mr Ravvenscrorft....Ravenscroft."

"Well, the special orifice of course, the special orifice you mentioned, Mr Song....Singh."

"Orifice?"

"You know, a hole, a mouth, a nostril, an earhole, a bum hole. And of course women have an additional orifice. Someone once said - though not me I assure you - it's so they can piss and moan at the same time."

More pregnant silence for a moment or two then Mr Singh said, "I just want simply to tell you all about our new digibox, Mr Ravenscroft."

"Then please do, Mr Singh, please do. But it can't be all that good if it's got a hole in it. In which case I won't be requiring one; I have more than enough trouble with the one you have already supplied me with and it is hole free."

Despite sounding very confused Mr Singh was adamant. "There is no hole in our new digibox, Mr Ravenscroft; I can say that with complete honesty."

"It is hole free?"

"The new Talk Talk digibox is hole free."

"Definitely definitely?

"Definitely."

"Good. So how much extra per week is it? And don't say it's free, with the idea of slipping another fiver onto my monthly payment hoping

I'll miss it, like you people have a habit of doing."

There was another pause, obviously while Mr Singh was thinking tactics, then he said, "I am an honest man, Mr Ravenscroft. It is another ten pounds per month only. And for that you will get...."

I will never know what I would have got because it was time to start getting my evening meal ready, so I politely thanked Mr Singh for his trouble, said goodbye, put the phone down and left him free to pester someone else.

****

August 26 2017. *MR. & MR.*

Atkins and I would never have asked the Reverend Lachie to marry us if Atkins hadn't had such a bad experience whilst swimming with seals.

We had travelled to Scotland to complete two of his 'Ten things I want to do before I die' list. We had done the first, a railway trip on the West Highland Line from Fort William to Mallaig. It had gone perfectly except for when Atkins, hoping to ingratiate himself with the ticket collector - although he claimed he was just trying to be friendly - remarked to her that she reminded him of Nicola Sturgeon. I have never seen a Scottish wildcat in the flesh but if its snarl is any fiercer than that which the ticket collector turned on Atkins I would be very surprised. It was followed by a stream of invective I felt sure was mostly swear words but was delivered at such speed and in a such a heavy Scottish accent that I struggled to make out a word of it, although I would bet on 'Sassenach bastard' being in there somewhere.

After staying overnight in Mallaig, and enjoying an evening in a pub that boasted over a hundred malt whiskies (and trying not a few of them), we had moved on to the Isle of Mull, where Atkins hoped to swim with dolphins. On arriving there all was as expected; yes, there were dolphins to be found in the area, yes it was possible to go out in a boat to see them, and yes, provided you could get near enough to them, you would be able to swim with them. From amongst the several boat owners offering dolphin-spotting services we picked Dougan *"But ye can call me Doogie"*, Atkins feeling that his having a beard and looking a bit like Captain Birdseye probably meant he was a better sailor than the others. I remarked that it could also mean he was better at selling fish fingers but Atkins chose to ignore this. I also mentioned that I would be happier in one of the larger boats on offer, to which Atkins's reply was that Dougan's craft was the least expensive and as he was paying for it how happy I felt about it didn't enter into it. Soon after first light - a time which Dougan assured us would provide us with the best opportunity to see and swim with dolphins - we embarked on his outboard motor-powered rowing boat and set out into the deep blue Atlantic. Taking Dougan's advice, which was advisable inasmuch as my swimming lessons had so far only taken me to the 'proficient at the dog paddle stage', I wore a life jacket. *"I shall have tae charge ye five poonds for the lend of it, mind, but better tae be safe than sorry,"* Dougan had warned.

Much sooner than I expected we were among sleek grey shapes swimming, leaping, diving through the water. "Dolphins ahoy!" shouted Atkins excitedly.

"Seals," said Dougan, to Atkins's disappointment. "Nae but seals, laddie. There'll be nae extra charge," he added, probably because before setting out he had relieved Atkins of another tenner for the petrol, incidentally bringing his fee up to that offered by the other, larger and more comfortable boats. *"Did I no mention that fuel was nae in with the price?"* Dougan had said with a straight face. I remember thinking that we probably wouldn't be far out to sea before he produced a bottle of whisky and offered us a compulsory 'wee dram' at some outrageous price.

"The seals are nice, aren't they," I said appreciatively. "Quite spectacular close up."

"Lovely creatures," said Dougan, and then, with great confidence, "And where there are seals ye can pretty much guarantee ye'll soon be seeing dolphins."

Atkins perked up immediately. "Really?" He got to his feet. "I'd best prepare myself then."

He began to strip down to his hired wetsuit. (He had put his normal clothes on over the top as it was still quite chilly at that time in the morning.) Now although the sea was by no means like a mill pond by no stretch of the imagination could it be described as choppy - which Atkins later claimed - but whatever it could be described as it didn't help Atkins when, in the act of trying to disengage his trousers from round his ankles he stumbled and fell overboard. By the time

Dougan had managed to turn the boat round we were fifty yards distant. In front of us, as we made our way back to Atkins, the sea was full of leaping seals and leaping Atkins. One of the seals must have escaped from a circus for it could clearly be seen trying to balance Atkins on its nose. The other seals seemed to be waiting their turn. I am sure I saw a couple of them oink and clap their flippers together in applause. A minute later we managed to drag the distressed Atkins, shivering with both the cold and fear, back into the boat.

Later, back at the hotel, Atkins was inconsolable.

"We can stay on an extra day and try again tomorrow," I suggested, trying to cheer him up.

"Are you mad?" said Atkins. "You're not getting me out there again. Bloody seals, they're bonkers."

"Perhaps that's why you don't get people wanting to swim with them like you get people wanting to swim with dolphins?"

"And can you bloody blame them?" Atkins put a hand gingerly to his back. "I think they must have thought I was a beach ball."

The following day, back on the mainland, Atkins having put Swimming with Dolphins on the back burner - probably never to return to the front burner the way he kept going on about it - we pulled up outside the little flint stone church. I noticed that, fortuitously, prominently displayed beside the arched entrance was a 'CHURCH ROOF APPEAL' sign along with a thermometer type thing which indicated how far away the appeal was from reaching its target (£10,000). Although I say it was fortuitous there was an ongoing roof appeal I wasn't at all surprised - few churches nowadays don't have a similar appeal going. Cynic that I am, I have long suspected that builders of churches are asked not to waste too much time on the roof specifically so that the vicar can sometime in the future have an appeal for its repair and perhaps divert some of the money donated to another worthy cause, such as his wine cellar fund. Be that as it may the church having a roof appeal might well be a useful negotiating tool for what Atkins and I had in mind.

The evening before, whilst reading the local weekly newspaper, an item of news had caught my eye. It concerned the Scottish Episcopal Church and their recent historic decision to back same sex marriages. Individual vicars would not be bound by this decision, however, and if same sex marriage failed to rock their font they could opt out. In particular the news item spoke of the vicar of one such church, who was not only against the union of two homosexuals, but was reported as saying, amongst other things, *"I would sooner chew my leg off than marry them."* As the church wasn't too far from the hotel in which we were staying I saw this as an ideal opportunity to rid Atkins of the foul mood he'd been in ever since the incident with the seals. It would cheer him up. And me likewise.

After the Reverend Lachie had invited us into the little cottage attached to the side of the church and we had introduced ourselves to each other he said, very pleasantly, "And wit can I dae for ye, gentlemen, this fine day?" (Excuse the 'wit', the 'dae' and the 'ye' but that's how they talk up there.)

I took Atkins's hand in mine, squeezed it and said, "Well if it isn't too much trouble, Reverend Lachie, we would like very much for you to marry us." I cast a fond smile at Atkins. "Wouldn't we, Rupert?"

Atkins batted his eyelashes, coyly. Princess Diana never batted her eyelashes more coyly. "I can't wait, Monty."

At that juncture we fully expected the Rev Lachie to send us packing, probably with a few choice words ringing in our ears to help us on our way. To test if his resolve held up when tempted with filthy lucre we would then offer to pay him well over the odds to perform the ceremony. That he had an ongoing roof appeal only strengthened our chances of becoming Mr and Mr Atkins-Ravenscroft, as in addition to the inflated marriage fee a hefty donation to the church roof appeal could be brought into play. Sadly, it was not to be.

"Why, it will be mah pleasure, mah absolute pleasure," the reverend beamed. "When would the ceremony suit ye? I'm quite free at the moment, quite free."

"Er....er...." was the best I could manage. Atkins couldn't even manage that.

"Is there a wee problem?" said the Reverend Lachie solicitously, noting this.

"No....no....it....it's just that we felt....that is, we read in the newspaper....we felt that you might be in some way opposed to same sex marriage."

Atkins found his voice. "According to the newspaper, 'Bloody pillow biters' was one of the expressions you used to describe homos."

"Describe *us*, Rupert means," I said quickly, "Describe *us*, not homos; Rupert made a slip of the tongue."

"Of course, a slip of the tongue, Rev," said Atkins. He laughed it off. "Me, a homophobe? I can't wait to get Monty between the sheets I can assure you." Just in case this wasn't enough to persuade the Reverend Lachie Atkins gave me the fluttering eyelashes treatment again and patted my bottom.

"Ah've had a re-think since I said that," said the reverend. "After a long talk with mah bishop ah've seen the error of mah ways, nae matter what the goode book has to say on the subject. Just a wee matter of misinterpretation, ye understand." He rubbed his hands together in anticipation. "So when would the ceremony suit you fine boys?"

"Not today," said Atkins like a shot. "Definitely." Having said it he sought a reason why. "There's the best man, Mary, to organise. And the bridesmaids, Alf and Bert. They'll have to travel up from England."

"So it will be, say, maybe a week, a week to ten days from now," I added.

"Nae problem, just as ye say. I'll see you then, then," said the Reverend Lachie.

Needless to say, he won't. To quote the Reverend Lachie, I would sooner chew my leg off.

****

Sept 1 2017. *THE MASTER SPECIES.*

The other day, after reading a 'Is there life on Mars?' article, I took to wondering what a couple of Martians might make of life on Earth if they were to look down on us from their spaceship hovering high above. Perhaps it would be something like this:-

DAVE MARTIAN: "From the countless species of life we have come across on this planet of Earth it is quite obvious which of the Earthlings are the big cheeses, which of them is the master species."

STEVE MARTIAN: "It is?"

DAVE: "Well of course. The human beings. I mean they've worked everything out. How to make fire, how to grow food, how to use the fire to cook the food, how to build nice warm houses in which to eat the food and to shelter themselves from the elements. They've invented cars and boats and aeroplanes in which to travel, both at home and abroad, they've invented sports to play, they've invented the cinema, TV and the theatre to entertain themselves, they've invented leisure parks, museums, swimming pools, books, magazines and newspapers to amuse and inform themselves, opera, ballet, rock and roll, pole dancing, porn, the lot. Yes, human beings are the master species all right."

STEVE: "What about dogs?"

DAVE: "Dogs?"

STEVE: "I reckon dogs are the master species."

DAVE: "Dogs? Are you joking?"

STEVE: "Not at all. I mean take work. A human being has to go to work most days to earn money to buy food and to spend on all the other things he needs. The dog doesn't have to go to work to earn money to buy food. The human being feeds it. All the dog has to do is lie around all day licking its bollocks and daydreaming about its next tin of Pal and sniffing other dogs' bums when it gets half the chance. Maybe the dog will chase a few birds if it feels like a bit of exercise, perhaps it will bite the postman if it feels in the mood for a bit of fun, possibly it will bark loudly if it feels like annoying the neighbours. But only if it wants to. It doesn't have to. The dog leads the Life of Riley."

DAVE: "That may well be true. But a dog doesn't get to go, for instance, to the cinema."

STEVE: "A dog doesn't want to go to the cinema. Why would it? It wouldn't be able to understand what the people in the film are saying. Dogs only understand words like 'fetch' and 'down boy' and 'stop trying to shag my leg'. Those expressions don't come up too often in your typical Hollywood blockbusters. All a dog wants to do for its leisure is go for a walk. Which brings me to another reason why I think dogs are the master species."

DAVE: "Which is?"

STEVE: "Who takes the dog for a walk? The human being. The bloke who owns the dog. He doesn't want to take the dog for a walk, he doesn't enjoy taking the dog for a walk, he's tired, he's been at work all day earning money to buy food for the dog. It's the dog that enjoys going for a walk. The dog *loves* going for a walk. It especially loves the bloke throwing a stick for it while it's out on the walk. The bloke doesn't like throwing the stick. Ten minutes of throwing the stick and he's had enough, he's knackered. The dog isn't knackered, the dog is still full of it, it's been lying around all day, it has energy to spare, the dog is still very keen on more stick throwing and if the bloke stops throwing the stick it will bark its fool head off until he starts throwing it again. So, tired or not, when he comes home from work, and soon to become absolutely knackered after about two hours' stick throwing, the bloke has to take the dog for a walk. Otherwise he's being cruel to the dog; and if he's cruel to the dog someone might report him to the RSPCA, and then he's for it big time. So he takes the dog for a walk. Which brings me to another reason why I believe dogs to be the master species."

DAVE: "Why is that?"

STEVE: "Well sometime during the walk the dog will have a shit. Who clears up the shit? Who has to pick up the shit in a little black plastic bag, designed expressly for that very purpose, and carry it about with him for the rest of the walk? Not the dog. The bloke. It's the bloke who has to carry the bag of shit, either swinging it gaily as if he couldn't care less about the embarrassment of having to carry a bag of dog shit around with him, or trying to hide it behind his back in the hope that people won't see him carrying a bag of dog shit around with him. If he had any sense, instead of throwing the stick for the dog to chase, he'd throw the bag of shit and the dog would get a mouthful of shit when it clamped its jaws on it, but then he'd be in trouble with the RSPCA again. And although what you said about the achievements of human beings is true, when you bear in mind what I have just said about their relationship with dogs then clearly they are subservient to dogs, therefore I think I'm safe in saying that on the planet Earth dogs are the master species."

DAVE: "I think you're right, Steve. I'll put it in our report."

****

Sept 4 2017. *FOUR IN A BED.*

Four in a Bed is a reality television game show screened every weekday on Channel 4. It consists of four pairs of B&B owners who take it in turns to stay with one another and pay what they consider to be a fair price for their stay, irrespective of the real price. The winner is the B&B adjudged to be the best value for money. On arrival, and having been shown their room for the night and advised as to the cost, the respective teams then inspect the room, picking up on anything untidy or not reaching the standard expected. The following morning they each fill in an anonymous form telling the owners how they feel about their room (its cleanliness, facilities, quality of breakfast, etc.) before stating if they would stay there again. They also pay the owners of the B&B an undisclosed amount of money, in a sealed envelope, based on their valuation of the room; if they believe it's worth the money they pay in full, if it isn't they underpay. On the final day, after each B&B has been visited, the respective hosts undo the envelopes. The team getting the highest percentage of what they charge for their rooms are declared the winners.

I watch *Four in a Bed* with my daughter Carol-Ann, who calls on me every day since The Trouble died. We enjoy the programme immensely. Our enjoyment though, is derived not from watching the show itself but in trying to pick, after the opening episode, which of the contestants will turn out to be the biggest arsehole; not always an easy task as more often than not they are all in the running.

Anyone who hasn't witnessed what these B&B owners get up to in an attempt to win the competition would be hard pressed to believe it. In the search for dust - a must during the Cleanliness of the Room section - more than one contestant has donned white gloves before running their finger tips along the top of the door frame. Same with the lampshades. (One couple brought along a small set of steps with them to enable them to do this.) *"While you're up there, Betty, check the inside for dead flies."* Inspection of the cleanliness of the bedding - primarily in the search for hairs and stains on the sheets, but anything untoward will do - is exhaustive. I have seen a magnifying glass used. Often the sheets are declared *"Nowhere near the same quality as ours, and they're charging a lot more than we do."* Several times I have seen flashlights produced to aid the search in dark corners for spiders and signs of mice. Nothing is safe from prying eyes in the search for imperfections, something, anything, that might offer up an excuse to mark down the room and thus increase their own chances of winning. The bowls of WCs receive special attention. Operating theatres aren't examined as thoroughly. Woe betide a brown stain within! *"Two points off for that, Michelle, it could be anything."* Often a folded piece of toilet tissue pinched between finger and thumb is ran around the inside rim in a search for the black gunge that can collect there over a period of time. Shower waste outlets are lifted out, the inside of them examined minutely. The *inside* of them. *"Look at this, Herbert. Disgusting. Hair. Slimy soapy gunge. Two points off for that at the very least."* Why anyone, having seen the behaviour of these awful people on TV, would want to spend a night in their B&B is quite beyond me. No it isn't. I wanted to. I've been wanting to for some time. To give them a bit of their own back. And I did, last week.

As luck would have it Carol-Ann and I had already planned a few days in the Yorkshire Dales, so it all fitted in quite nicely. A few weeks before our trip we had seen one of the very worst of the awful B&B owners in action. We will call her Mrs Waterhouse, and the name of her B&B the *Shoulder of Mutton*, as to use their real names might cause problems. But everything else is true. Mrs Waterhouse and her husband Des, who was nowhere near as awful as his wife but did nothing to rein her in, had won their competition easily. The *Shoulder of Mutton* was the first of the B&Bs to be visited and, as is usually the case, the other three couples, not knowing what marks they themselves would be getting when it was their own turn to be assessed, had gone easy with their marking. During the subsequent days Mrs Waterhouse, taking full advantage of this, had gone to town. In response to Mrs Jeffries comment that Mrs Waterhouse's choice of bedroom wallpaper was a bit on the bland side Mrs Waterhouse said that the Jeffries' wallpaper had given her a splitting headache, she still had it, she hadn't slept a wink all night, but this was partially due to the lumpy mattress, and even if she had managed to get to sleep she would have been woken up by the constant stream of heavy traffic outside from about 5 a.m. onwards. A mark of 3 out of 10 ensued. In response to Mr Davidson's revelation that he had found a dead spider in the bottom of the wardrobe Mrs Waterhouse had stated that she had found three spiders, still living, in her wardrobe, and another spider, thankfully dead, under one of the pillows. A mark of 2. She was just as vicious when it came to settling the bills, knocking at least thirty per cent off each.

Carol-Ann and I checked in to *The Shoulder of Mutton*, two rooms at £70 a night including breakfast, no discount for single occupancy. Mrs Waterhouse showed us to our rooms. We said they were lovely. Five minutes later I went down and caught Mrs Waterhouse. "Er, Mrs Waterhouse?"

"Yes, what can I do for you, Mr Ravenscroft?"

"It's just a little thing about the room, tiny, hardly worth bothering about...." I stopped and looked at her closely. "Don't I know you?"

She frowned. "I don't think so."

"I'm sure I've seen you before. Just a minute....weren't you in *Four in a Bed* on the telly? You were! You were on not long back!"

"Guilty," she said innocently, with a little

smile.

"You won, didn't you."

"We did have that honour, yes."

"Paid in full by everyone, as I remember. Still, you must have been quite confident; a B&B of this quality at the price you're charging."

"Des and I like to think we tick all the boxes."

"And I'm sure you do, Mrs Waterhouse; it is quite evident. Well, nice talking to you, I'll see you at....oops, I almost forgot what I came down to see you for."

"Yes?"

"Perhaps it might be better if I showed you?"

Back in the room I let her have it.

"Well it's the dust mainly."

Mrs Waterhouse's head shot back in surprise. "Dust? Where?"

Where? Everywhere. Carol-Ann and I had made sure of that. We'd brought a bag of it with us (along with a bag of hairs, a jam jar of slimy soapy gunge, a jar of black gunge, and a dozen assorted spiders) and had made generous use of it on top of the door frames, on top of the wardrobe, in the wardrobe, on the skirting boards, in and on the lampshades. I informed Mrs Waterhouse of this and had her check it out. She was completely bemused, not to say crestfallen.

"I....I don't understand. I checked the room myself only this morning."

I spread my arms and shrugged. "What can't speak can't lie. However it isn't only the dust that gives me cause for concern. Apart from the many hairs in the bed there's a suspicious-looking stain on one of the sheets." Well there is now.

This really set her back on her haunches. "What!"

"I won't mention the wadge of hair contaminating the underside of both the washbasin sink plug and shower water outlet (put there by me of course), but I will mention the state of the WC."

"What's *wrong* with the WC?"

"Nothing, if you're prepared to ignore the black gunge under the rim of the bowl and the fact that it has recently been used, and whoever used it neglected to flush it." (Me again.) "And as if all that isn't bad enough my daughter's room is exactly the same." I turned to Carol-Ann. "Isn't it, my lovely?"

"Well no, Dad" said Carol-Ann, "to be honest. Although it *is* true there's dust all over the place, hairs in the bed, a stain on one of the sheets, and I have gunge where you have gunge. However nobody has recently used the lavatory and failed to flush it. But they did piss on the board."

I hadn't told Carol-Ann to say someone had pissed on the board; she had gone off script and come up with it herself, much as Atkins often does on our little adventures. Perhaps something of my friend had rubbed off on her during their recent assignation? Or perhaps it's just that she's a chip off the old block.

Mrs Waterhouse left, totally befuddled and not far from tears. The following morning I handed her an envelope.

"What's this?"

"Payment for our night's stay."

She opened the envelope, took out notes and counted them. Four twenty pound notes and one ten. She was aghast. "You've underpaid me by fifty pounds!"

"Think yourself lucky, it would have been sixty pounds if I hadn't forgotten the rats."

****

Sept 10 2017. *A SEX SHOP TALE OF OUR TIMES*.

There is a saying that truth is stranger than fiction. I used to think this was the case, until I read, or read as much as I could stand without either falling asleep or losing the will to live, of *The Lord of the Rings* - a sad hour of my life that never got the chance to be happy - and that put the kibosh on it for me. Never, in a million years, could the truth be stranger than that. However....

I once wrote a TV sketch set in a sex shop, featuring a vicar as one of the clients, not for one moment imagining that something like it was ever likely to happen. The vicar was played by Rowan Atkinson, and an excellent job he made of it. The sketch started off with Rowan breezing merrily into the sex shop and telling the assistant behind the counter, in a very loud voice, and to the embarrassment of all the other customers, that he would like to buy a tin of Rampant Bull Jelly, *"A very large one please as I am feeling especially rampant today."* A highlight of the sketch was when the vicar introduced himself to one of the shop's customers, played by Pamela Stephenson, and offered his hand for Pamela to shake. Pamela, pushing a supermarket shopping trolley jam packed full of sex aids of every description, responded, forgetting that she had a dildo in her hand at the time, and the vicar ended up shaking not Pamela's hand but the dildo, much to their mutual discomfort. All good clean fun then.

Yesterday, more than thirty years later, whilst out on a rare shopping trip, I noticed a vicar entering the Stockport Merseyway branch of Ann Summers. A moment then, in a way, of *deja vu*. I followed the vicar in. What on earth did a man of the cloth want from a sex shop? See-through surpluses for the choirboys? Crotchless cassocks? I had to know.

Unlike the vicar in my sketch this vicar didn't breeze up to the counter, but nor did he show any signs of embarrassment. I fell in behind him as an assistant appeared at the counter. She smiled. "Yes sir, can I help you?"

"I'd like a dildo, please," said the vicar.

The assistant didn't bat an eyelid, possibly because vicars were far from unknown amongst the shop's customers. She pointed. "There's a selection over there."

The vicar set off. The assistant turned her attention to me. "Can I help you, sir?"

"I'm shopping for the same thing," I said, and set off after the vicar.

The display of dildos on offer was large, as were most of the dildos. The vicar picked up a big black one, looked it up and down, gripped it tightly at the shaft end, raised it in the air and brought it down sharply. He did it again and grunted with satisfaction. He saw me looking at him. "Mislaid my bobby's truncheon," he offered, with a friendly smile.

I raised an eyebrow. "Oh?"

"I live alone," he explained. "I've always kept a police truncheon on my bedside table at night to fend off any potential intruder. But it went missing when I had the decorators in last week and I haven't seen it since. Try as I might I have been unable to obtain a replacement. I asked at the police station but they said they don't use truncheons anymore, they use a night stick, but even if they had a truncheon they wouldn't let a member of the public have it, despite my telling them what I intended to use it for."

I commiserated. "Miserable sods."

"Anyway I happened to mention it to my verger and he mentioned it to a friend and the friend suggested that a dildo might do the job as adequately as a truncheon, so here I am."

I thought to ask him if by any chance his decorators had been women called Roz and Caz, probably with short haircuts, who might well have other ideas for the use of the truncheon, but I doubt he would have understood what I was getting at so I didn't bother.

He raised the dildo again and brought it down hard into his cupped hand with a resounding thwack. He nodded approval. "Yes, that should do the business."

"It would certainly give an intruder a headache."

"It would indeed." His brow furrowed. "What is its real purpose, by the way?"

"Ornamental rubber bell-ended beer pump," I said, quicker than you could say Jack Robinson or artificial cock.

"Well, nice talking to you," said the vicar, and set off back to the counter to pay for his purchase. Then I got out of there before someone who knew me came in.

So maybe some things are stranger than fiction, or at least as strange.

****

Sept 14 2017. *THE BIG ONE.*

"It looks a lot higher close up. I didn't realise it was as high as that."

'It' was The Big One on Blackpool's famous Pleasure Beach. The person who didn't realise it was as high as it is was Atkins. I turned to him and said, "You're not going to chicken out again, are you?"

"Of course I'm not."

"Because it isn't an aeroplane, you know. You don't have to jump out of it."

"I was simply saying it was higher than I expected it to be," said Atkins, testily.

"I mean you've already chickened out twice."

"I am *not* going to chicken out!"

The first time Atkins had failed to complete, due to cowardice, one of the ten things he wants to do before he dies, was at the tattoo parlour.

He was all for it when we went in. *"Just wait till I show it off down at The Grim Jogger, everyone will want one."* I expressed doubt that the landlord, who has only one arm, might like to keep his remaining upper limb free from tattoos, or at least, instead of having the Niagara Falls tattooed on it, might plump for a bottle of Stella Artois in an attempt to drum up a bit of trade. There was never any danger of me having a tattoo of course; I had gone along because I'd never seen a tattoo being done live, plus I wanted to see if the tattooist could do a decent job of Niagara Falls with a man on a barrel going over it. Originally Atkins had said he might have a man *in* a barrel going over it, but on the way to the tattooist's parlour I suggested it would look a lot better, much more adventurous, more gung-ho, if the man was *on* the barrel, astride it as though it were a bucking bronco. Atkins congratulated me on an excellent idea.

When we arrived at the tattoo parlour the tattooist assured Atkins that his requirements wouldn't be a problem, he'd done much more difficult tattoos, and mentioned a crossword puzzle enthusiast who had had his penis tattooed in a crossword design. Atkins asked what was so difficult about it, adding that he imagined a man going over the Niagara Falls astride a barrel would be a much sterner test of the tattooist's skills. The tattooist replied that although he had tattooed the crossword successfully, and to the customer's satisfaction, unfortunately he hadn't left enough space for the clues. The customer had insisted he wanted them; it wouldn't be a proper crossword if it didn't have clues. After the tattooist had come up with what he thought was a reasonable solution - to tattoo the clues on the customer's balls, one Down, one Across - the customer had turned down the suggestion point blank. *"It would be like having the crossword in the Star and the clues in the Daily Sport,"* were his words, according to the tattooist, who then had to remove the tattoo completely and start all over again with a smaller crossword.

Atkins was next up and the tattooist, who was already halfway through tattooing somebody and had broken off for a minute to welcome Atkins, disappeared back into a cubicle and continued tattooing whatever work of art he was currently engaged in, hopefully not another crossword puzzle or we could be there all day. Soon we heard a buzzing sound not unlike a dentist's drill, but louder, and almost immediately after a startled scream. Atkins was out of there like a shot.

Outside, when I managed to catch up with him about a hundred yards down the street, I told him that a bit of discomfort was to only to be expected. Atkins replied that screams like the one he'd heard didn't come from someone who had experienced a bit of discomfort, it came from someone who had experienced a lot of discomfort, not unlike someone who had just had his throat cut. I suggested that perhaps the tattooist had accidentally hit a bone. Atkins said there was no way the tattooist was accidentally hitting one of his bones, and that was that.

Regarding the second of the ten things he'd already chickened out of, I thought at first he had gone through with it. *"It was a wonderful experience, quite exhilarating, even more exhilarating than the time I rubbed noses and a few other things with that Eskimo in her igloo when I went on that trip to see the Northern*

Lights," were his words, when I asked him how the parachute jump had gone. Yes, he had been tied to the front of an experienced parachute jumper as promised, no the experienced jumper had not tried to molest him on the way down, he was still a virgin in that department. It was only a couple of days later when his daughter Esther rang to ask if he was round at my house as she couldn't locate him and had urgent news for him that the truth came out. He hadn't done the parachute jump at all. Esther had ferried him to the aerodrome as he *"might be a bit shaky after the experience and might not feel like driving"* and the next time she saw him was not floating to earth on the end of a parachute but climbing sheepishly out of the aeroplane with the parachute still strapped to his back. When I later questioned Atkins about it he said it was merely a bit of stage fright, purely temporary, that he had re-scheduled the jump, and had only told me he'd already done it as he had every intention of doing so. I asked him if he had a spare sack of salt he could let me have as it would take far more than a grain to swallow such a blatant lie. We left it at that but I'm pretty sure he hasn't done anything about arranging another jump.

Now, nearing the front of the queue for our ride on The Big One, Atkins suggested we should perhaps hold on for a bit to let our stomachs settle. I said that it was over three hours since he'd had his fish and chips and if they weren't settled now they never would be.

We made the batch of people for The Big One's next car. "I'm not sitting at the front," said Atkins, as it pulled up and discharged its passengers. "You could easily tip out when you're going down, there's nobody in front to stop you."

"We'll sit at the back then."

"I'm not sitting at the back! It's even worst at the back than it is at the front, there's a danger of whiplash at the back."

"Is there anything wrong with the middle? Could the well of a car in the middle perhaps be knee deep in rattlesnakes? Could the only seat available to you be between two tattooists?"

Atkins chose to ignore my sarcasm and we boarded the car somewhere in the middle. For the next couple of minutes, as we rode The Big One, Atkins, eyes madder than a White Walker on acid, hair on end and not just from the slipstream, clutched my arm in an iron grip and screamed his head off. Apart from that I quite enjoyed the experience.

"Good, that, wasn't it," I remarked, once we'd alighted and left The Big One far behind us.

"Wonderful."

"You can let go of my arm now." Shamefaced, Atkins released his grip on me. "We'll do it again in a bit if you like," I said.

"No! No, once is enough, thank you, I've done what I wanted to."

"Perhaps when your stomach's settled?"

"It's already settled."

"Vomiting your fish and chips over the side would have helped."

"Yes well that's all behind me now, isn't it."

"I think some of it is behind the Funhouse too."

Atkins stopped and eyed me balefully. "Will you just *stop* it!"

I allowed bygones to become bygones. I put a friendly arm around his shoulder. "Come on, mate, let's get you home. There's our trip to United to plan; I don't want anything going wrong with that. We are still going, are we? You're not going to chicken out of that too?"

"I'll be there, you can count on it; I wouldn't miss it for the world."

****

Sept 16 2017. *PORN.*

In the newspaper today was an article by an 'expert' on teenage matters. She was advocating that much more could and should be done to prevent websites showing pornographic material *'as it could ruin teenagers' development into responsible adults'*. She made the point that the more often young people sought out online porn the more likely they were to have a 'recreational' attitude towards sex; that they would tend to specifically view sex as a purely physical function such as eating or drinking. She put forward a powerful case, one I am in complete agreement with. But having done so she ended the article by saying *'that any teenager has only to type into a computer search engine the word 'Porn' and they would instantly be confronted by dozens of pornographic images'*, thus informing any teenager who didn't already know this. Talk about shooting yourself in the foot? But was it as easy to access internet porn as she was making out?

I typed the word 'Porn' into Google. There were 2,150,000,000 results. I clicked on the top result, '*Free Porn Videos & Sex Movies - Porno, XXX, Porn Tube and Pussy.*' A second later a row of four thumbnail screens the width of the page showing people engaged in various sorts of sex flashed onto my computer screen. I scrolled down the page. There were twelve such rows, forty-eight little screens in all. At the bottom of the page I found I could go to a further ten pages, plus. In the interests of research, as they say - especially certain rock stars who have been caught downloading illegal porn - I scrolled slowly back to the top of the page, taking in each screen. I have never felt so white in my life. Nor as under-blessed; much as a chimpanzee might feel in a land of gorillas. (In fact there was a chimpanzee in one of the films on offer, *Zo(e)o Time*, but only in a minor role; it was turning somersaults with a banana in one hand and its dick in the other whilst watching the head zookeeper having it away with Zoe, a young girl zookeeper.) But I'm getting ahead of myself.

At least eighty per cent of the men taking part in the sexual gymnastics were black. They say that size isn't everything but in the case of one of the men it very nearly was everything. What a penis! He was a really skinny little bloke, only about five feet tall, and by the sound of his accent - his opening words were *"Lit's git you fucked, Doll."* - probably an aboriginal Australian. If he had posed sideways with the words 'TO MELBOURNE 200 MILES' tattooed on his erect penis he could have passed for a signpost. In fact you could probably write 'TO MELBOURNE 200 MILES' on his penis.

In contrast to the multiplicity of black men in the films the vast majority of the women were white. The whole website could have been called *The Black and White Shagging Show*. In the three pages I scrolled through only one white man was having sex with a black woman. It was a ten minute epic called *Mandongo*, supposedly about a white cotton plantation owner. He was dressed in a Panama hat, open-neck white shirt, and riding breeches - well to begin with; he ended up in just the hat whilst coupling with one of his slaves in the cotton fields.

It all reminded me of the only other time I have watched porn films, back in the early 1980's. At the time I was writing for the comedy sketch show series *Alas Smith and Jones*, starring Mel Smith and Griff Rhys Jones. Amongst other things I wrote for them were several of their 'Head to Head' sketches, studio pieces in which Mel and Griff sat opposite each other, their chins cradled in their hands, and talked about this and that, in much the same way that Peter Cook and Dudley Moore had done a couple of decades previously. Anyway, Mel and Griff decided they wanted to put out an LP record of the same, but, freed from the constraints of good taste that television demanded (or did at the time), they wanted it to be a lot more near the knuckle, more 'adult'. The LP would be called *Scratch and Sniff*. Along with other Smith & Jones scriptwriters I was asked to contribute. I decided to write something about how porn films are made - I had no idea how they were made, but I did know how films were made and I knew how to have sexual intercourse (although not in some of the variety of ways I was soon to discover). To this end I visited one of the many places in Soho showing porn films at the time. Despite my lack of a dirty raincoat I was allowed in without question by the girl at the ticket desk. There were about ten people dotted about the darkened fifty-seater theatre, all of them sitting as far away from each other as possible, all avidly with their eyes glued to the screen. I don't think they even noticed me take my seat. After each short film, all of about ten minutes' duration, there was a five minute break before the next film. I was only in the place for about an hour and during these five minute breaks every man in the theatre visited the toilet, some of them twice, and I don't think it was for a pee. I can't say I enjoyed watching the films - to this day I can't appreciate what people see in them - to me it was more a frustrating experience than a pleasurable one, much like being shown a film of people eating fried fish and chips and not being able to have some for yourself.

Having watched four of the films I had seen enough to be able to put something together. I have forgotten most of the script I subsequently wrote and my complimentary copy of the LP went astray long ago, but the following is a bit I remember. (In fact *Scratch and Sniff* is still available on Amazon, both in the original vinyl and as an audio CD, but I'm too mean to buy a replacement, and anyway I have never much liked watching or listening to my own stuff.)

SCRATCH AND SNIFF EXTRACT.

MEL: I mean what you see on the screen in these porno movies isn't what *really* goes on.

GRIFF: No?

MEL: You know how the blokes are always good-looking with a toned body and that?

GRIFF: Yeh?

MEL: Well it isn't *their* dick you see doing the business. What you see on the screen, in the build up to the actual shagging, is the good-looking bloke. But when it gets to the shagging part they bring on another bloke, one with a dick as big as a donkey but too ugly to be seen doing the shagging. You never see the good-looking bloke with his dick out. At the point he takes it out of his trousers they cut to a close-up of the ugly bloke taking his dick out of an identical pair of trousers. You never see the ugly bloke, you only see his dick; but the audience thinks it's the good-looking bloke who's doing the shagging.

GRIFF: Yeh, I know.

MEL: What?

GRIFF: My brother does a bit of acting in porno films. Our Darren.

MEL: The one who's the spitting image of you?

GRIFF: Yeh.

MEL: He won't be the good-looking bloke with the toned body then?

GRIFF: Right. His missus, Darlene, she's got a job in porno films too.

MEL: Go on?

GRIFF: Yeh, they often work together. She's an

oooh-er.

MEL: What, you mean like she's a prostitute?

GRIFF: No, an oooh-er. And an aaah-er. She does, like, the passionate noises of pleasure, the ooohs and ahhhs, for a girl who's being shagged who's not very good at doing them herself. Darlene makes a better job of it; apparently she's very good at making passionate noises of pleasure while she's being shagged.

MEL: Well she's been shagged a lot, ain't she, your Darlene, she's had a lot of practice. She was the school bike. (SOUNDS PUZZLED) I can't remember her making any passionate noises of pleasure when I shagged her.

GRIFF: Yeh well you haven't got a big dick, have you.

****

Sept 18 2017. *MAN U v EVERTON.*

"Are you going like that?" I said unbelievingly, on opening my front door to Atkins. He was wearing a Manchester United shirt with 'Atkins' on the back, a red and white bowler hat perched atop a red curly wig, two United scarves, one round his neck, one tied around his midriff, and a huge red and white rosette.

Atkins seemed surprised. "What's wrong with me?"

"You're not going to paint your face red and white then?"

"I don't want to go over the top."

"You're just an armchair United supporter.

Surely you don't watch them on the telly dressed like that?"

"What? Who do you think I am? No, they're my grandson Norbert's. Named after the great Nobby Stiles of course. My lad George was a great fan of his. Norbert can't go today; he has to do some more of his one hundred hours community service."

I didn't ask what Norbert had done to deserve the imposition and Atkins didn't offer it, although I'm sure it wasn't because of any embarrassment at his grandson's behaviour; Atkins is quite incapable of being embarrassed. The reason for my friend's eccentric dress, of course, was that we were about to fulfil another of the ten things he wanted to do before he dies. On seeing the state of him I half wished he'd died before he got this far. I just shrugged and got on with it. "Have you got the tickets?"

Atkins patted his back trousers pocket. "Safely in here."

"You'll be all right will you? The seats aren't right at the back? I don't want you refusing to sit in them because they're too high up."

"I've been to see the doctor about that. He said I might be developing vertigo."

"So we could be in trouble?"

"No. Well we'll still be on the ground won't we, in a manner of speaking. Apart from that the seats at Old Trafford won't be moving at about five hundred miles-an-hour like the ones on an aeroplane and The Big One."

"I'll get my coat."

It must be fifteen years since I was last at Old

Trafford. Up until then I had been a long-time season ticket owner, one of the few who didn't come from London according to the nonsense put about by the tenants of the Council House, Manchester City. I gave up my ticket soon after Sky TV rather than the Premier League authorities decided the fixture list and clubs stopped playing their fixtures on Saturday afternoons at three-o-clock and started playing them at any time other than Saturday afternoons at three-o-clock; twelve noon Saturday, four-o-clock Sunday, eight-o-clock Monday night and two-o-clock in the morning, Friday. I might have imagined the last one but I don't think it will be long before it happens. Since then I've followed United's matches on TV, usually at the pub. I even gave up on that a couple of years ago when the Dutchman Louis van Gaal seemed intent on transforming the Theatre of Dreams into the Theatre of Nightmares, but with Jose Mourhino in charge we've been doing a bit better of late.

We travelled down to Old Trafford on the train, arriving about an hour and a half before kick-off to give Atkins plenty of time to 'soak up the atmosphere' as he put it. Happily kick-off was not at two-o-clock in the morning Friday but four-o-clock Sunday. Included in Atkins's soaking up the atmosphere routine was a visit to the United superstore. I expressed doubt about their having anything on sale that he wasn't already wearing. He replied that on the way to the ground he'd seen someone wearing a sort of Roman centurion helmet in red and if one suited him he might exchange it for his bowler hat, in which case I could wear it, he was sure Norbert wouldn't mind. I told him that I would mind, very much.

Fortunately we didn't spot any Roman helmets in the superstore, so after browsing around for a bit and Atkins buying a face-painting kit as a gift for Norbert for loaning him his outfit, and just about managing to refrain from using it on himself, we made our way to the stadium. Getting quite close to the queues of fans entering I stopped. "Where are we going?"

"To our seats, where else?"

"This is the away supporters section."

"Is it?"

I held out my hand. "Give me the tickets." Atkins did. They confirmed my suspicions. "Where did you get them?"

"E-bay."

"We'll be sitting with the Everton supporters! We'll be completely surrounded by Everton supporters!"

"I suppose we will."

"You can't sit with the Everton supporters dressed like that!"

"Well I know that, I'm not daft."

"You're doing your level best to prove otherwise. You'll have to get rid of it all."

"I can't do that, it's Norbert's."

"Well you can't wear it, you'll get lynched. And me with you. We'll have to go back to the superstore and buy a holdall or something. You can stash it in there till after the match."

"And what am I going to wear if I do that?"

"Have you got anything on under your shirt?"

"Just my vest."

"It hasn't got a message written on it has it? 'Everton fans are scum' perhaps?"

"Well of course it hasn't; what do you take me for?"

"Don't tempt me. You'll have to manage in just your vest. I wouldn't worry about it, you'll be overdressed compared with some of the fans, most of them are naked to the waist nowadays. Come on, superstore."

We managed to find a plain holdall and with Norbert's United gear safely stashed away I gave Atkins instructions on how to conduct himself, once we had taken our seats, if we were to escape with our lives. I know my man. "Try to talk with a thick scouse accent," I advised. "It's all from the back of the throat, as though you're fetching up a green gob at the same time you're talking. Mention the bizzies at lot, Liverpudlians are always on about the bizzies. Remark that you nicked some nice hub caps last night. Don't say the words 'scouse and 'bastards' in close proximity to each other. And call me la when you speak to me."

"La?"

"It's what they say for 'lad' in Liverpool. *"Are you bleedin 'jokin', la."* Very similar to that. And remember. Remember this, above all, if you don't remember anything else. *Whatever* you do don't leap to your feet when United score. Remain firmly rooted to your seat. Shout *"Offside ref, bleedin' offside you blind bastard,"* or something similar if the mood takes you. But do not, DO NOT, on no account, leap to your feet."

Fortunately Atkins's vest wasn't red, but a colour that was once white, so didn't pose any problems.

I am delighted to report that both Atkins and I, surrounded by hostile Everton fans, managed to maintain our anonymity. For three minutes. Which was all the time United needed to score. I wouldn't like to say which of us was the first to leap to his feet, arms aloft in jubilation with a joyous cry of 'GOAL!' when Valencia's thunderbolt of a shot hit the back of the net but there couldn't have been more than a nanosecond in it. It was wholly instinctive of course, completely involuntary. I should have known - a football fan can no more fail to express excitement when his team scores than he could climb Mount Everest blindfolded.

I don't know the time gap between Atkins punching the air and the man in the seat next to Atkins punching Atkins, three seconds at the most. During this time a deeply hostile voice behind me spoke: *"What the fuck!"* At the same instant the shirtless fat man in front of me swivelled round in his seat. I have never witnessed such hate in a pair of eyes. Nor have I ever been so frightened. He cocked a thumb in my direction and spat out to the man sitting next to him, a huge broken-nosed presence with 'Rooney' tattooed in blue on his forehead, *"Can youse believe these two fuckers!"*

I will draw a veil over the next five minutes. Suffice to say that before half-a dozen stewards came to our rescue, bodily dragged us from our seats and deposited us outside the stadium 'for or own good', we had both been punched several times. Atkins had a black eye and a cut lip.

After we had checked there were no bones

broken Atkins said, "Shall we give it five minutes then try to sneak back in?"

I won't say what I replied.

****

Sept 24 2017. *ANNOYING.*

When BBC producer John Lloyd, whom I knew from *The News Huddlines*, was putting together a team of scriptwriters for *Not the Nine O'Clock News*, I was one of the writers he invited to contribute material. I asked him what sort of stuff he was looking for. He said: *"Write about things that annoy you."* It is by far the best advice I have ever been given; not only did I have some success with John's new show but I have been writing about things that annoy me ever since. (The Trouble was constantly telling me that it didn't take much to annoy me. I'm glad she was right because it's earned me a living for the last forty years.) Many of the pieces in this book were spawned by things which annoy me - *A Canvasser Calls, A Racial Slur, Celebrities, Chef, Computer Virus, Cyclists, Haka,* to name just a few. The three previous *Stairlift* books, many of the letters in *Dear Air 2000, Dear Coca-Cola* and *Dear Pepsi-Cola*, were generated by things that annoy me, as were many of the incidents in my novels. I've only just got over all the adulation surrounding Usain Bolt's appearance at the recent World Athletics Championships. For God's sake, all he's doing is running! I could run when I was one year old. All right, he's fast, but it's not as if he's doing anything along with the running; when I used to run in the Co-op Sports Day I had to carry an egg on a spoon, have one of my legs tied to someone else's leg, or have both legs in a sack. All this over the top hero worship goes for Mo Farah too; he wants to try running 10,000 metres with one of his legs tied to Lord Soames, that would slow him down a bit. And where were the headlines when Usain Bolt failed to come up to expectations? Where was 'SHOT HIS BOLT'? Very disappointing. I would have thought one of the red tops would have had that all over their front page. And where was 'SLO MO' when Mo only came second?

Here are just a few more of the many things that annoy me:-

Television news correspondents and reporters annoy me immensely. Why do they find it necessary to play an invisible concertina when they're talking to camera? Doing a report should be a simple matter. All you have to do is stand there and talk. But they can't do that; they have to play the invisible concertina while they're doing it. They start off all right, with their arms by their sides, as a normal person does when speaking, but immediately they start talking their hands move to waist level, about a foot apart, and start playing the invisible concertina. In, out, in, out, squeeze, squeeze, all the time they're talking. Why do they do it? I'm convinced they would be struck dumb if you tied their arms by their sides. Most other people manage to talk without doing it (I say most, because others on TV do it too, especially presenters). It wouldn't be so bad if you could *hear* the concertina - it could perhaps be playing a jolly Irish reel or some atmospheric French cafe music. This would not only have the benefit of making their report more entertaining but would help drown it out if they were spouting the usual inane drivel. Or perhaps, accompanying themselves on the invisible concertina, they could sing their report about the five-legged calf in the Yorkshire Dales? Or the Morris dancer assaulting a shopper in Tesco's car park with his shaker stick?

I have a theory why they play the invisible concertina. Almost without exception these people present their reports in mid-shot, i.e. from the waist up; you wouldn't even know they had hands if they didn't suddenly appear and start playing the concertina. I recall from the time I was a schoolboy that whenever we weren't using our hands to write with the teacher made us sit with palms down on the desk, so she could be sure we weren't playing with ourselves. So maybe it's something to do with that.

Here are a few more things that get on my pip. Along with what I would like to do about them if only I had the bravery or was handed the opportunity.

*

I am at the Glastonbury Festival, amongst thousands of others gathered at the Pyramid Stage. On stage are The Killers. I can hear them but I can't see them. I would be able to see them but for the fact that directly in front of me, obstructing my view of the stage, is a big fat arse. It belongs to a young woman who is sitting on the shoulders of her boyfriend/husband/whoever. Why do they do it? Don't they know that other people want to see too? Probably they do it the better to see. Just as likely they do it because they want to be seen. (It crosses my mind that the big fat arse is at my nose level, much like the arses of horses that pass me on the Sett Valley Trail. The only consolation is that it doesn't smell. But these are early days; in my experience big fat arses don't go very long before they let forth with big fat farts.) I can take some comfort, however, from the huge screens at the side of the stage on which one can watch the show. Or at least I would be able to if immediately to the left and right of the girl with the big fat arse are two more girls sat on their boyfriend/husband/whoever's shoulders. Their arses aren't as big but they are still big enough to obstruct my view of the screens. I have been here before. This time I come prepared. I take out the large hat pin I have brought with me for such an eventuality and ram it as hard as I can into the big fat arse. The owner of the arse screams and pitches forward over the head of her carrier and into the crowd in front of her. I can see The Killers! Go Brandon! When the girl returns, clutching her arse painfully, I slap my face hard with the flat of my hand, say *"Damned hornets"* and sympathise with her. Fearing another hornet attack she doesn't climb aboard her companion again.

*

I am poised at the wheel of a powerful 4 x 4, parked outside the entrance to a large caravan site. Hitched to the back of the 4 x 4 is a house on wheels. (A bricks and mortar house, not a caravan.) It is about thirty feet wide, as wide as the road. There is no way past me. It is early

Saturday morning, a popular moving-on time for mobile caravan owners. The caravan site is situated on a minor road leading to a motorway, five miles distant. When the first of the caravanners emerge from the site, towing their caravans, I start up my 4 x 4 and proceed down the road at two miles per hour, a speed not much less than the speed at which the drivers of cars towing caravans travel whenever I'm behind one. They can't pass me so, seething with frustration, they honk their horns for me to get out of the way, maybe by pulling into the nearest lay-by while they pass (unlike they ever do), but I ignore them. I reduce my speed to one mile per hour and smile a contented smile. Maybe I sing a happy song. The following day I do the same, but this time I'm towing a thirty feet wide horse box outside the exit road from a gymkhana.

*

"Would you mind getting me a pint of bitter while you're about it?"

The man who has elbowed his way in front of me in the queue at the bar turns to me with a scowl. *"What?"*

"You pushed your way in front of me."

"It's every man for himself in here, mate."

The above conversation actually happened. What happened next didn't, although it might do one day if ever I summon up enough courage. Maybe when I'm eighty.

"You pushed your way in front of me."

"It's every man for himself in here, mate."

I undo my topcoat to disclose that underneath I am a walking bomb. I open my hand to reveal I am holding a detonator. I speak loud enough for everyone at the bar to hear me. I look at my watch and say in a foreign accent *"In fifteen seconds I go up and the rest of the pub with me."* The bar clears in no time. I lean over the counter and help myself to a pint of bitter.

*

Arsenal have gone down one-nil after thirty seconds.

TV COMMENTATOR: And that is just the start Arsenal didn't want!

CO-COMMENTATOR (Me): Really? I'd have thought it would have been exactly the start they would want, going a goal down less than a minute into the game.

COMMENTATOR: And he's hit the post!

CO-COMMENTATOR: Well upon my soul! So that's why the ball didn't go into the net and bounced back into play! I never would have guessed in a million years!

COMMENTATOR: It's a goal!

CO-COMMENTATOR: You do realise that we're not on the radio, do you Clive? I mean we're on the telly, the audience can actually see what's happening on the pitch.

COMMENTATOR: And Danny Wellbeck should really have done better from three yards out with an open goal in front of him.

CO-COMMENTATOR: *And there was me thinking he was doing quite well by hoofing the ball into Row Z!*

COMMENTATOR: *And Harry Kane has got options on his left and options on his right.*

CO-COMMENTATOR: *You mean Spurs have two players called Options?*

And then of course you get the post match interview.

"With me now is the hero of the match, Paul Pogba. Tell me, Paul, how enjoyable was it not only playing out of your skin and scoring the winning FA Cup final goal here at Wembley but completing your hat-trick at the same time?"

"Well actually it wasn't at all enjoyable. In fact I'd far rather have played absolute shite and missed three sitters."

*

"And next on the tee here at Palm Springs on this wonderful day is Bobby Bubba, a swell golfer and just a really nice man, as I'm sure you'll agree, Corey."

"A really nice man, Dave. Bobby has a lovely wife, Clarissa May. I met her at the PGA. What a sweet, charming gal."

"She is indeed, Corey. Bobby and Clarissa May are just a really nice couple."

"Couldn't wish to meet a nicer couple, Dave."

The above is a typical exchange between two

American golf commentators. No human beings annoy me more than these purveyors of pap, men who seem to live in a world where everything is nice, every golfer is nice, no one is a shithouse, everything in the world of golf is hunky-dory. Or as they would say, *just* hunky-dory. I have been unable to do anything about it before, but this morning I have been gifted the power of magic.

"And next on the tee here at Palm Springs on this wonderful day is Bobby Bubba, a swell golfer and just a really nice man, as I'm sure you'll agree, Corey."

"Bobby is two under par at the moment, Dave."

"Bobby has a lovely wife, Clarissa May."

"One shot behind the leader."

"Bobby and Clarissa May are just a really nice couple."

"I believe Bobby knocks Clarissa May about a bit, Dave."

"They have two lovely children, Bobby junior and Betty Lou Sue."

"Bobby beats up on Clarissa May real bad."

"Just really nice kids, too. Betty Lou Sue is the spit of her mother and Bobby tells me that Bobby junior is already on the way to following in his illustrious pop's footsteps."

"Beats the shit out of Clarissa May, Dave."

"Well I'm sure that if Bobby does beat up on Clarissa May, Corey, which I find a little hard to believe to tell you the truth, Bobby being just a really nice man, that he beats up on her in just a

really nice way."

"Gave Clarissa May a black eye last week, Dave. Punched her real hard, gave her just a really black eye."

"I'm sure that must have been an accident, Corey."

"Blacked Clarissa May's other eye the following day, Dave. And broke her nose. Smashed it to a pulp."

"Well they do say accidents come in threes, Corey."

"And the day after that he chopped both her legs off."

"That's what I mean about Bobby. Such a considerate man. In addition to being really nice. I mean he'll now be able to push Clarissa May around in a wheelchair, won't he, what with her having no legs; show all the world how much he loves that sweet gal."

"He killed her, Dave. He murdered Clarissa May. Put a bullet clean between Clarissa May's eyes."

"That's Bobby's love of Clarissa May shining through again, Corey. You see by Bobby putting the bullet where he did you wouldn't be able to see the bullet hole, what with the two black eyes and smashed up nose. And now Bobby's playing partner today, Hal Swenk the Third, steps up onto the tee. Hal is just a really nice man."

****

Sept 28 2017. *THE CLEANING LADY.*

My osteopath and good friend Martin Davies had treated me for a bad back. To ensure his work had the best chance of success Martin had advised me not to bend or lift anything for at least two weeks. Enter Mrs Marchington, a cleaning lady. She came to me without recommendation, but according to her advert in the newspaper shop window did 'EXSELLENT WORK, £9 PER HOUR, SATISSFACTION GARANTEED'. As Mrs Marchington's advert was the only one in the window for cleaning ladies, and in the hope that her cleaning was better than her spelling, I engaged her.

Some years ago The Trouble and I employed a cleaner on a temporary basis. On the morning she was due to start her first day I was awoken at around 5 a.m. by the sounds of The Trouble cleaning the house from top to bottom *"Because I don't want to give that cleaner the chance to spread it about I have a dirty house."* There was no chance of that happening with me. I didn't lift a finger for the four days prior to the arrival of Mrs Marchington. No carpet hoovered, no tidying up done, no kitchen swept and waste bin emptied, nothing.

Today was her first day. She arrived on time, a good sign. She was a small, thin woman, aged about fifty. On removing her topcoat to reveal that underneath she was wearing a flower-patterned wraparound overall she would have been a dead ringer for Hilda Ogden had she been wearing a turban. I was just grateful I didn't have a flight of pot ducks on my wall or a 'muriel' that might distract her from her work. As I remember, Hilda Ogden spent about ten per cent of the time cleaning the *Rover's Return* and ninety per cent gossiping. To ensure that Mrs Marchington couldn't do the same my plan was to go for a walk while she attended to her cleaning duties.

"A couple of hours we agreed, I believe?" I said.

"We shall have to see about that, I didn't realise it was as big as this," she said, glancing around the room as if it was the O2 arena. "And I have to mention I don't do hoovering."

"You don't do hoovering?"

She touched her back and winced. "Bad back. Large nerve roots are shot according to the hospital. I've only got to look at a hoover and my back's off. You wouldn't believe the pain."

"I see." Not so much in sympathy for her, more in the hope she might take pity on me and perhaps put up with the pain for a bit whilst she did just a bit of light hoovering I said, "I'm suffering from a bad back myself at the moment." I touched my back and winced even more than she had.

"You'll know how I feel then. And why I don't, *under any circumstances*, do hoovering."

I smiled a defeated smile. "Perhaps you'd like to start in the kitchen? There's plenty non-hoovering work to be done in there."

She looked hesitant.

"What's the matter?"

"Does this plenty to be done involve emptying the kitchen bin?"

"And replacing the full bin liner with a new one, yes. You'll find a supply under the sink."

"You see I might struggle there. If it's heavy. Only if it's heavy, mind. But what full bin liner isn't heavy?" She put a hand to her shoulder. "Acute biceps tendinitis. If I accidentally let my own kitchen bin get too full I have to get the man next door to empty it."

I thought to ask her if he'd perhaps drop round and empty mine but didn't think there would be much chance, so I just shrugged and said, "Well I'm not sure how heavy it is, but if it's too heavy for you I'm sure I'll be able to make other arrangements." Then I added, with a touch of sarcasm in my voice, "In fact I think my friend Tyson Fury might be dropping by later." Utterly wasted.

I thought about what other cleaning needed to be done. I was about to ask what she was like at dusting, half-expecting the answer that she couldn't do dusting because the dust got on her chest and caused her to cough violently, causing collateral damage to her back and shoulder, when I recalled a joke told by Ronnie Corbett in his armchair spot in *The Two Ronnies*. This was the part of the show where Ronnie told a short joke, or 'funny story' as he liked to call them, which he extended to five minutes or more by shooting off at tangents before returning to the joke. This particular funny story, without the tangents, went as follows. *A man knocked on the door of this house. The lady of the house came to the door. The man tipped his hat politely and said, "I'm a handyman, looking for work. Have you any odd jobs you need doing?" The woman thought for a moment and said, "The back door needs painting. You could do that." The man said, "Sorry, I don't do painting. The fumes get on my chest. Have you anything else I could do?" The woman thought again and said, "There's wood out the back to be chopped into logs for the fire?" The man said, "Sorry, I don't chop wood. Bad back. Have you got anything else?" The woman thought yet again. "The back garden needs tidying up?" The man said, "Sorry, I don't do garden tidying. Gives me vertigo when I bend over." The woman looked him up and down and said, "You say you're a handyman. You don't do painting. You don't chop wood. You don't tidy gardens. What makes you think you're handy?" And the man said, "Well I only live round the corner."*

Now, paraphrasing the woman in Ronnie Corbett's tale, I said, "You can't hoover, you can't lift anything heavy, you'll probably have a reason that prevents you from dusting, what makes you think you're a cleaning lady?"

I half expected her to say 'Because I only live round the corner' but she just jutted out her jaw, as though daring me to disagree, and said, "Because I *am* a cleaner."

I was a bit disappointed with her answer, to tell the truth, and contented myself by saying "You could have fooled me", paying her up and telling her not to bother coming again.

Whilst writing the above I recalled that I myself once had hopes of writing Ronnie Corbett's armchair spot. It was at the time that Spike Mullins, who had been writing it for years, announced he no longer wanted the job. A replacement for Spike was needed. Sample monologues were requested from writers eager to take on this task. I was one of the lucky ones. My funny story was about a couple who went for an evening walk in the countryside. Part of it went: *"....it will do me good to get out of the house," said the woman, "I've been tied to the Aga all day." To which her husband replied, "Well of course you have, it's the only way I can get you to cook." Not that she was much of a cook. When attempting to boil an egg one day she burned the water. In fact she was so bad that her husband arranged for her to take a Cordon Bleu cookery course. She returned after the first lesson with a shepherd's pie she'd made. He told her it should have been cordoned off. Anyway, back to the walk in the countryside. As they made their way past open fields the husband, Geoffrey we'll call him, but really his name was Bruce Lee - not Bruce Lee the Kung Fu man, but two separate forenames, 'Bruce' and 'Lee'- he was half Australian, half Chinese, came from Alice Spring Rolls - and if I were to call him Bruce Lee it might confuse you. Because it's already confusing me and I've got a script. Bruce Lee emigrated to the Cotswolds with his parents, whilst still a boy, hence his knowing all about the countryside. Thought I'd better make that clear in case you thought I was telling fibs about him coming from the countryside, for the purpose of the joke. Which I was. Anyway, as I was saying, Geoffrey pointed out various countryside items of interest to his wife, Sandra we'll call her - because she was called Sandra - as they'd only just moved to the country from London and she, unlike*

Geoffrey, was unfamiliar with many of its rural charms. "That's a Friesian," Geoffrey said, pointing to a cow. "And that cow there, the very light brown one, that's a Jersey. That one there is an Aberdeen Angus; you can tell by its tartan udder." No he didn't, I just made that up. "And that one there is an Ayrshire." And Sandra said, "And what sort of cow is that? The smaller, white one?" "That's a sheep," he said. I told you she was unfamiliar with the countryside, didn't I. In fact the only time she'd seen lamb before there was mint sauce on it. Anyway, back to the story. By now the light was going, which coincided, perhaps due to the country air, with Geoffrey starting to feel a bit randy. "Sandra, my sweet," he said, "How about we climb over the wall into that field and make love? There's not a soul about and it's almost dark, no one will see us." And Sandra, being a bit of a sport - which is perhaps her saving grace because she can't cook - said, "I'm up for that, Geoffrey." So they clambered over the wall, get down in the field and start to make love. Soon Geoffrey said, "Sandra, love, you haven't got a torch with you, have you? Only I can't see what I'm doing properly." And she said. "You've no need to tell me that, you've been eating the grass for the last five minutes."

Ronnie didn't use my funny story. I can't think why. David Renwick, who went on to write *One Foot in the Grave*, got the job. A far better writer than I, he made an excellent job of it.

****

Sept 29 2017. *The End?*

Well that's it. Another *Stairlift* book finished. I don't know if there'll be another, but I hope so. If there is I will probably call it *Stairlift to Heaven 5 - The Old Bugger Finally Pops His Clogs* and have it published posthumously. In the meantime Atkins and I are off to China in a few weeks time to walk part of the Great Wall. If I can get him on it, that is. Because after the debacles with his parachuting ambitions and the Big One he'll probably say it's too high and chicken out. I will then suggest we call in at the nearest garden centre to take in the terracotta plant pots, as if we went to Xian to see the Terracotta Warriors he would find them far too frightening. We shall have to see.

****

Terry Ravenscroft's latest novel is The Ring of the Lord. Following is the first chapter.

The Middle-earth shire of Dreg, in the Gondor region, was to be found in an area known in our times as Derbyshire, with the addition of the less salubrious part of Cheshire and the less inbred part of Yorkshire.

A millennium before this book begins, the Dark Lord paid one of his infrequent visits to the shire of Dreg, just one of many shires and regions he ruled over with a rod of iron clasped in a fist of steel. On arriving he was not best pleased with what he saw. He was even less pleased upon further investigation; he was not pleased with the way the Dregs conducted their affairs and he was not pleased with the way they conducted their lives. He took no time at all in taking them to task on what he considered to be a sorry state of affairs and warned them that if they didn't mend their ways, and with great haste, there would be trouble. He would return in a year's time to confirm that they had mended their ways. He returned a year later. They had not mended their ways. There was trouble. The Dark Lord chose not, on this occasion, to unleash his terrible power on the Dregs - he only resorted to his terrible power as a last resort - but even so he still brought to bear swingeing changes in the current lifestyle obtaining in Dreg. Their previous life of decadence and debauchery became a thing of the past, and soon the good and wholesome peace of long ago returned to the shire. (Just one of the things the Dark Lord put paid to was the wanton extramarital sexual intercourse indulged in by the Dregs. In the Dreg of today there is no sexual intercourse at all. Now, if a Dreg married couple - and *only* a married couple - want a baby, they simply wish for one by the light of the full moon and the following morning they wake up to a baby in a wicker basket on their front doorstep. Now, a thousand years on, they have no memories of sexual intercourse. Which isn't to say that some of the populace don't experience sexual feelings; they do - but having got the sexual feeling they have no idea how to further it to its natural conclusion.) Of course the Dregs didn't take kindly to the new regime imposed on them, a good and wholesome peace coming a poor second to a life of decadence and debauchery, but at least it was better than having the terrible power of the Dark Lord turned on them. Which would spell the end. Literally. But time, as the saying goes, is a great healer, and within a few hundred years all memory of their former lifestyle had been lost in the mists of time. And is where this book begins.

PART ONE

5030 B.C.

CHAPTER ONE

The Quest

Tunnbledemere, the chieftain of Dreg, rose from his ceremonial throne and slowly approached his son Draybweevil. From his robes he produced a silver pendant which he offered to Draybweevil, saying, "Take this sacred pendant, my first born."

Draybweevil's jaw dropped in astonishment. He knew of the sacred pendant but had never seen it before. It was all he expected and more. A long moment passed as he admired its great beauty, then he tore his eyes away, looked deep into the wise, wizened face of his father, a picture of himself in years to come, and said, "The sacred silver pendant of Goz!"

Tunnbledemere smiled fondly at his blond-haired son. "Put it on, good Draybweevil."

With trembling hands Draybweevil took the sacrosanct solid silver pendant and placed it round his neck.

"You are safe from all danger now," said Tunnbledemere.

The two men, with a number of selected Dregs, were ensconced in Tunnbledemere's secret lair. The dank, dark cave, illuminated by torches of tarred willow kindling, sharp stalactites thrusting down from its lofty ceiling like witches teeth, was deep in the foothills of the Very Foggy Mountain. (When the Very Foggy Mountain was first discovered, on a rare not-too-foggy day, it had originally been named the Foggy Mountain; it was only some years later, when an expedition to conquer its peak couldn't find it, that it was re-named the Very Foggy Mountain, Dregs being sticklers for accurate descriptions of the shire's geographical features.)

"It will help protect you throughout your perilous journey through the Underworld to.... who knows where? Perhaps through Sablon, through Zariam, through Xerezz and Onandonandonandon," Tunnbledemere continued.

Draybweevil's ice-blue eyes were already afire with zeal. His breathing quickened. "And my quest, Father?"

"In truth there are two quests, my son. You will of necessity need to successfully complete the first before you can accomplish the second." Tunnbledemere took a moment to survey the forty or so important Dregs forming a rough semi-circle around him. "As you are all well aware, many years ago, way beyond the memory of any of us assembled here today, the Dark Lord erected an invisible impenetrable barrier around the perimeter of the farthest reaches of Dreg, making it impossible for anyone to leave the shire and travel to other shires and lands beyond. You will also know that the invisible barrier, even though preventing people leaving, does not preclude them from entering, although, as they can never return from whence they came, no one ever does, the rare exceptions being those who have recently had a peesashite (the Dreg equivalent of a solicitor) move into the house next door. We are, to all intents and purposes, completely cut off from the rest of the world." Tunnbledemere looked at his son in earnest. "Your first quest then, Draybweevil, will be to somehow find a way out of Dreg."

"Perhaps an attempt to scale the wall?" said Draybweevil, after a moment's thought.

Tunnbledemere shook his head sadly. "I'm afraid such an attempt would prove to be no more fruitful than any of the previous attempts."

Tunnbledemere was correct in his judgement. And yet, if one were to stand at the wall and toss a stone in its direction to a height of not less than six feet, it would plop down on the other side. The problem arose when someone attempted to scale the wall. For having reached a height of six feet they would discover that the wall had increased in height to seven feet. And when they had climbed a further foot they would find it was now eight feet. And eight feet became nine, and so on and so on. The highest height ever attained in attempting to climb over the wall was by a giant, who scaled it to a height of two hundred and thirty feet, at which height he happened to look down. A tragic mistake, as it turned out, as it brought on an attack of vertigo, whereupon he fell off. Up to the present time the wall had caused a hundred and fourteen deaths, a hundred and thirteen of them when the person climbing it had fallen off, the other one when the giant fell off and landed on a passing elf. A goblin with more ambition than sense had once tried to pole vault over it, in the hope that the quick execution of the art would take the wall by surprise. The wall was not surprised, the goblin smashed into it with great force, and became the ninety-eighth of its victims. Another goblin brought up the hundred when he tried to reach the other side by means of a giant catapult.

Tunnelling under the wall had been attempted almost as many times as climbing over it, but with a similar lack of success. For as the height of the wall increased the further one scaled it so its depth was added to the further one dug down.

Now, Draybweevil placed a strong, reassuring hand on his father's shoulder. "I will do my utmost, Father. Or die valiantly in the attempt."

Tunnbledemere smiled fondly at his handsome son. "You would not be the son I know you to be if that were not true, brave Draybweevil."

"And the second quest, Father?" said Draybweevil, anxious to get things underway. "Is it perhaps to find out why the sky at night is filled with little yellow objects which some call stars?"

"No, it is not that, Draybweevil."

"Then perhaps it is why the sea is blue? For I know that many Dregs would like to know the answer to that enigma; I would like to know myself, it is a question that has intrigued me for all my young life."

Tunnbledemere shook his head again. "Not why the sea is blue either. Much, much more important than that. In fact the most important quest ever to be undertaken by a Dreg," he said gravely. Tunnbledemere was seldom less than grave since the Dark Lord, apparently on a whim, had brought to bear his terrible power on the neighbouring shire of Drool, and in a matter of minutes completely laid it to waste. Nothing had escaped from the terrible power; every living thing, every human being, every animal, every bird and bat of the air, every insect, everything of fur and feather, every creature of the lakes and rivers, every tree and bush, every flower, every blade of grass. Everything that had ever lived was rendered lifeless. Few had borne witness to the Dark Lord's terrible power and lived to tell the tale. Of those who had, none knew how he generated his power. But they had seen that he did, and to disastrous effect. So these days, days which now seemed longer than they had before the Dark Lord's evil deed, Tunnbledemere's responsibilities as chieftain lay as heavily on his shoulders as on the shoulders of the oxen that daily ploughed the fields of the shire. For what the Dark Lord had done to the shire of Drool he could just as easily do to the shire of Dreg, if ever the mood should take him.

"The second quest, Father?" prompted Draybweevil, when Tunnbledemere, dwelling on his troubles, didn't continue immediately.

Tunnbledemere paused a moment before speaking his next words. His tone was solemn. "It pains me to place such a great responsibility on your young shoulders, Draybweevil."

"Young shoulders they may be, Father." His back stiffened. "But broad enough I'll vouchsave."

Tunnbledemere nodded then took the deepest of breaths, as though to invest his words with the seriousness he felt they deserved. "Your quest then, Draybweevil, is.... *nothing less than to find out why everyone in fantasy novels has a silly name!*"

A collective intake of breath came from all those present that fateful day. Gasps of awe, of wonder, of trepidation, were forced from the throats of Binglebang, of Meelamoola, of Bootyscoot, of Snotwangler, of Fartwurgler, of Bumsucka, of the dwarf, Arselow, of the goblin, Vakyoomkleena, of the elf, N'Safety, of the troll, Socialmeeja, of the giant, Economysize, of the wizard, Ovoz, of Condom the Protector, of Tampon the Absorber, and last, but by no means least, from Man With Very Long Name Who Has Been Given A Very Long Name Simply Because A Long Name Fills Up At Least Half-a-dozen Lines Every Time It Is Used And Is Absolutely Guaranteed To Be Used Many Many Times Because Almost All Fantasy Novels Are About As Thick As A Brick And The Few That Aren't As Thick As A Brick Are At The Very Least Six Hundred Pages Long And Therefore Using A Very Long Name A Lot Will Fill Up About A Hundred Pages And Thus Save The Author The Bother Of Thinking Up Even More Padding Than He Already Will Be Doing.

Draybweevil brow knitted in a puzzled frown. "But why do you wish to know this, Father?"

"If I have this information it will help to ingratiate myself with the Dark Lord, whose real name is Bleedintosspot, a name he detests with all his heart and soul," said Tunnbledemere. Always conscious of what had transpired on the Dark Lord's last incursion into Dreg, now brought sharply into focus by what had happened more recently in Drool, Tunnbledemere wanted to be as well prepared as was humanly possible should he ever return. "A name he hates so much that he has vowed to bring down a terrible punishment on the man responsible for bestowing silly names on characters in fantasy novels. So any assistance I can render to him in this ambition may help prevent him wreaking upon us the fate he inflicted on the Drools. It is a little insurance." The explanation over Tunnbledemere made to return to his throne, but stopped, remembering something. "Incidentally, Draybweevil, when you are on the quest there is one more thing I would like you to do for me. It the answer to a question which has always fascinated me. I am an old man, my time on Middle-earth will soon be over, and I would dearly love to know before I die."

Draybweevil placed his forearm across his heart. "I will find the answer to that question for you, Father."

"You are aware of the deep interest I have in fantasy novels?"

"It is an interest shared by many Dregs; indeed I am prominent amongst them. What is it you wish to know?"

"It is why the protagonists in such novels are always having strange, disturbing dreams."

Draybweevil gasped. The previous night, no sooner had the caressing but insistent arms of Morpheus dragged him reluctantly into a deep sleep - reluctantly because Draybweevil loved every single moment of his waking hours in his beloved Dreg and sleep to him was a deprivation of life itself - he himself, not for the first time, had experienced a strange, disturbing dream. Was the dream a portent of things to come? In his dream there were unforgettable visions of unfamiliar buildings with peculiar signs hung on their front elevations; 'Red Lion', 'Queen's Head', 'Rose and Crown.' A huge red and white banner attached to the front of the Red Lion read 'SKY SPORTS HERE!' Through one of the windows, in what appeared to be some sort of giant magic glass, about five feet by four feet in our measure, a game unfamiliar to him was being played. It involved two teams chasing around madly and kicking some sort of sphere, possibly a pig's bladder, much to the huge enjoyment of the many thousands of spectators watching, many of whom raised cheers and chanted loudly and boisterously throughout the action. All the spectators had seats to sit on, but unaccountably all were standing up. In a second magic glass another game involved a white-clad figure throwing a smaller red sphere at another white clad figure armed with some sort of wooden weapon-cum-shield, with which he attempted to either ward off or attack the sphere, whilst a dozen or so more white-clad figures looked on, several of whom yawned from time to time. In a third, a game similar to the one taking place in the first magic glass, involved bigger, more muscular men, who, when not fighting each other, were mostly throwing, rather than kicking, the pig's bladder.

Through the doors of the Queen's Head a young man and a young woman now staggered.

The young man had a swastika tattooed on his cheek, a bone through his nose and sported on his head a peaked cap worn back to front; the young woman had the words '*Too Drunk To Fuck*' emblazoned on a skimpy blouse that seemed designed to reveal, rather than conceal, her bulbous breasts. The word 'Fuck' was unfamiliar to Draybweevil. As the couple staggered and reeled on their way, with raucous cries of "*All police are bastards*" and "*We don't give a shit*" directed at no one in particular, pausing only to vomit on a passing cat and urinate in someone's front garden, they passed four people of a similar age. They were all smoking and drinking something called 'Carlsberg' from a bottle. However the mixture they were smoking couldn't have been the bat dung and dried weasel entrails rolled up in a dock leaf enjoyed by the majority of the Dreg race, but some other concoction, a mixture that apparently rendered those smoking it glassy-eyed, unsteady on their feet and totally incoherent. As the young men swigged greedily on their bottles a young woman, naked but for an even skimpier blouse than that worn by the first young woman, a thin band of some sparkly material girding her loins, staggered by on shoes that looked to have six inch nails in place of heels.. As she did they took pleasure in jeering at her. There was a cry of "*Slag*" from one of them, a cry of "*Show us your tits*" from another. The girl stopped and bent over, displaying her naked bottom in their direction. Continuing on her knickerless way she passed another young man slumped on the ground, a wretched-looking individual who appeared to be trying to push a small glass tube into his arm. Next to him, an older individual, a sad-looking wretch of a man, was inhaling a white powdered substance up his nose from the back of his hand.

The dream came to a sudden end when a sort of oxen-less cart with 'POLICE' emblazoned on the side suddenly appeared on the scene, klaxon blaring, and raced at high speed past both the young couple and the four smokers before screeching to a halt outside a building bearing the brightly-lit legend 'Pizzaland', whereupon two bulging at the waist fat-faced hungry-looking black-clad figures leapt out and rushed inside with cries of *'I'm having a king-size meat feast!'* and *'I'm having the same with double chips!'*

As Draybweevil's recollection of the dream ended Tunnbledemere was surveying the whole gathering. He said, "So, who amongst you will join brave Draybweevil on his quest, a mission in which he will in all likelihood have to slay the forty-headed dragon of Fannydoodle, the three hundred 6 metre high cage fighters of Titt, and the Seven Giant Rays of Bog, in addition to many more wholly improbable foes he will no doubt encounter on his way through the Discworld, the Carpetworld, the Slimmingworld, the PCworld, the Disneyworld, the Gardenersworld, and all the other worlds he may have to pass through if he is to arrive safely in Onanonanonanon, and, having made it that far, manages to discover why we have all been given silly names?"

"Surely we all will join him, Tunnbledemere," said Man With Very Long Name Who Has Been Given A Very Long Name Simply Because A Long Name Fills Up At Least Half-a-dozen Lines Every Time It Is Used And Is Absolutely Guaranteed To

Be Used Many Many Times Because Almost All Fantasy Novels Are About As Thick As A Brick And The Few That Aren't As Thick As A Brick Are At The Very Least Six Hundred Pages Long And Therefore Using A Very Long Name A Lot Will Fill Up About A Hundred Pages And Thus Save The Author The Bother Of Thinking Up Even More Padding Than He Already Will Be Doing.

Author's note. As this is a Kindle version of The Ring of the Lord, Book One, Dreg, and all Kindles being only as thick as a Kindle no matter how many times you repeat things in the texts of the many novels contained therein, Man With Very Long Name Who Has Been Given A Very Long Name Simply Because A Long Name Fills Up At Least Half-a-dozen Lines Every Time It Is Used And Is Absolutely Guaranteed To Be Used Many Many Times Because Almost All Fantasy Novels Are About As Thick As A Brick And The Few That Aren't As Thick As A Brick Are At The Very Least Six Hundred Pages Long And Therefore Using A Very Long Name A Lot Will Fill Up About A Hundred Pages And Thus Save The Author The Bother Of Thinking Up Even More Padding Than He Already Will Be Doing, will in future be known as Man Etcetera. Of course his name will be written in full in the hardback and paperback versions of this epic tome, thus fulfilling its purpose.

"I for one will certainly join him," said Bumsucka.

"I would deem it an honour to accompany him, Tunnbledemere," said Economysize.

"You can add my name too," said Man With Very Long Name Who Has Been Given A Very

Long Name Simply Because A Long Name Fills Up At Least Half-a-dozen Lines Every Time It Is Used And Is Absolutely Guaranteed To Be Used Many Many Times Because Almost All Fantasy Novels Are About As Thick As A Brick And The Few That Aren't As Thick As A Brick Are At The Very Least Six Hundred Pages Long And Therefore Using A Very Long Name A Lot Will Fill Up About A Hundred Pages And Thus Save The Author The Bother Of Thinking Up Even More Padding Than He Already Will Be Doing, Junior, the son of Man Etcetera. (*Sorry, couldn't resist that, Author.*)

Printed in Poland
by Amazon Fulfillment
Poland Sp. z o.o., Wrocław

19526509R00147